How to Really Love
Your Angry Child

How to Really Love Your Angry Child

ROSS CAMPBELL, M.D.
WITH ROB SUGGS

David C Cook
transforming lives together

HOW TO REALLY LOVE YOUR ANGRY CHILD
Published by David C. Cook
4050 Lee Vance View
Colorado Springs, CO 80918 U.S.A.

David C. Cook Distribution Canada
55 Woodslee Avenue, Paris, Ontario, Canada N3L 3E5

David C. Cook U.K., Kingsway Communications
Eastbourne, East Sussex BN23 6NT, England

David C. Cook and the graphic circle C logo
are registered trademarks of Cook Communications Ministries.

Unless otherwise noted, all Scripture is taken from the *Holy Bible, New International
Version*®, *NIV*®. Copyright © 1973, 1978, 1984 International Bible Society. Used by
permission of Zondervan. All rights reserved. Other quotations are taken from the THE
NEW ENGLISH BIBLE (NEB), copyright © the Delegates of the Oxford University
Press and the Syndics of the Cambridge University Press, 1961, 1970. Reprinted by per-
mission; the *Authorized (King James) Version* of the Bible (KJV); *The New Testement in the
Language of the People* (WMS) by Charles B. William,© 1966 by Edith S. Williams, used
by permission of Moody Press, Moody Bible Institute of Chicago; *The Holy Bible in the
Language of Today* (BECK), © 1976 by Mrs. William F. Beck; The Message (TM).
Copyright © 1993, 1994, 1995, 1996, 2000, 2001, 2002. Used by permission of
NavPress Publishing Group; New Living Translation (NLT) copyright © 1996 by Tyndale
Charitable Trust. Used by permission of Tyndale House Publishers.

Library of Congress Cataloging-in-Publication Data
Campbell, Ross, 1936-
How to really love your angry child / by Ross Campbell, with Rob Suggs.
p. cm.
ISBN: 978-0-7814-3914-5 (pbk.)
1. Child rearing–Religious aspects–Christianity 2. Anger in children–Religious
aspects–Christianity I. Suggs, Rob. II. Title.
BV4592.C34 2004
649'.1–dc21
2003010071

Reprint Editor: Susan Martins Miller
Interior Designer: RJS Design
Cover Photo: © Getty Images

Printed in the United States of America
First Edition 1995
First revised edition printed in 2003

5 6 7 8 9 10

091908

9564

Contents

Introduction

Dear Parents,

Nothing in the world is more important to you than the way you raise your children. You realize that the greatest joy—and the greatest anxiety—in life comes from the great task of training children to be strong, honest, and happy adults whose lives are marked with integrity.

If you didn't feel that way, you wouldn't be reading this book. And if you weren't greatly concerned with the problem of anger, you would not have selected this book.

You and I both realize we live in a world filled with unbridled anger—not just in children, but in adults. I share your concern about the world our children are preparing to enter. Because I have counseled hundreds of parents over the years, I know how burdened you can feel at times, how isolated, how frustrated. I know that anger can be a great issue in your life, too.

If you didn't feel a certain amount of anger, you wouldn't have your eyes open. There is plenty in the world to upset us these days—in the headlines, in the movies, in the very halls of our schools and churches. As we see all these problems and crises, we realize that mishandled anger is at the root of nearly every one of them.

Why? Because no one can rightly handle anger without being taught. The correct skills don't come naturally. Mature anger management must be taught at home, but it is not happening in many homes today. As you look around your community at some of the families you know, you will realize many people have bottled-up anger; they simply don't know what to do about it.

Anger, you see, is a little understood emotion—why we feel it, how we express it, and what to do when it takes hold of us. We must teach children how to cope, but we cannot do so unless we have first learned the great lessons ourselves. As you read this book, you'll find yourself thinking not only about the emotions of your children, but your own, those of your spouse, and perhaps those in the household where you grew up. Anger is a central issue in the lives of every one of us from the womb to the tomb.

It's about time you and I face the issues squarely and decide how we will manage them from here on out.

This book will help you understand exactly what anger is and how we express it. You'll be surprised by some of the answers. We will discuss the stages of our children's lives and how anger manifests itself at each juncture, each bend in the road. We will discover some practical actions to take when we face anger in our homes. And, I hope and pray, you will find some light at the end of that dark tunnel. You'll discover that, tough as this problem is, there are solutions; there are realistic reasons for optimism; and there are days ahead when you will realize that all your hard work as parents paid off.

You'll never live a life devoid of anger. The Bible tells us that we will be angry, but not to sin in our anger. This book will help you realize that anger and the response to it are two different things; and therein lies hope for happy, productive lives for us and our children.

Ross Campbell, M.D.
Signal Mountain, Tennessee
2003

1

Anger Comes Home

It all started for Nicholas, of course, when he was a toddler. There were the usual symptoms of the "terrible twos"—screaming tantrums when he was denied this toy or that shiny object. Friends and relatives assured Mom and Dad that Nicholas was "just going through a stage" that he would naturally outgrow. Unfortunately, family life for the Smiths took more unpredictable turns.

Nick's fits of temper lingered and even worsened as the boy progressed through childhood. He stopped rolling on the floor and pounding the carpet with his fists, but he expressed his fury in other ways. He continued to cry loudly, even in public places; he talked back; he slammed doors and sulked. The parents began to refer to these episodes as "Nick's meltdowns." As he moved into his elementary school years, teachers expressed concerns about class disruptions, and conferences were embarrassing.

Nick's father particularly suffered, because he knew exactly where the "temper genes" had come from. The last thing he wanted in life was to watch his son learn some of the hard lessons life had taught him about living with a short fuse. So he began to keep a close watch on Nick and his meltdowns. At the first sign of an episode, Nick's dad would bark, "Don't start!" Nick would seem even more frustrated and begin to stammer an objection. Dad's tone would become even more stern: "Stifle it!" Finally, Nick would be sent to his room with dire warnings about what would happen if he slammed a door, kicked a wall, or muttered under his breath.

Somewhere around the age of 11, the meltdowns began to subside. Life became more quiet in the Smith household. All the same, Nick's parents felt a strange intuition about the state of their family. Something wasn't quite right. Even before entering the predictable adolescent rites of passage, Nick was withdrawing into himself, shunning family activities whenever he was allowed. Then he was suspended for a few days from school after being caught pulling a fire alarm and disrupting the entire building. The principal made it clear that Nick was suspected of certain other furtive pranks that were troubling the school. They recommended counseling, but Nick's dad argued that the school was unfairly singling out his son for unfounded accusations.

Then came the shoplifting incidents. At first it seemed possible to imagine that Nick simply had made some poor friendship choices, but the last two incidents happened when he was alone. As Nick passed his sixteenth birthday, his parents reached out to him every way they knew how—but they were no longer certain they knew their son at all.

Nick's character profile is a composite of countless children I have met over the years. His parents are the same loving, concerned Mom and Dad I've helped over and over. The issue, of course, is anger and its management. For most of my career as a family counselor, I've been deeply concerned about the rising power of buried anger in a generation of children coming of age. I observed that many or most families in today's world had no real comprehension of how to deal with anger in children, and I knew that the poor handling of it could lead to nothing but disaster.

I would imagine that as a parent you take a great many precautions in your home. You're careful to store toxins and poisons in a safe place. You take care to know where your child is at all times. Perhaps you even regulate what kinds of television programs your child views and what sorts of computer activities may take place.

But are you aware that the greatest danger of all is the anger that dwells inside your child; that the most toxic poison out there is an unchecked, unbridled rage simmering within?

Give the matter some thought and you will realize that anger is an everyday issue, and it enters every frustrating circumstance of your child's life. If much of that anger is mishandled and misdirected, it will not simply dissolve and disperse. It will rise up in some form and damage or even destroy the child who harbors it—now or at some point in the future.

I believe this is precisely what we are seeing in our world today. As children come of age, they take their anger into the pressure cooker worlds of schools, social spheres, workplaces, marriages, churches, and families, where the damage is compounded. Take a close look at any entry on that list—church, for example—and you will realize that angry personalities are bringing turmoil at unprecedented levels. I work with an organization that nurtures ministers who have been insensitively handled and terminated by their congregations, and I can tell you that the misdirected anger of parishioners is at the heart of the problem. What about the workplace? We see the same situation. We live in a world spinning out of control because of points of anger that might have been arrested and properly treated at some point in the past.

The Problem of Power

We see the violence in the schools, but gun-related incidents are only the tip of the iceberg. This problem is far more pervasive, and the only people capable of solving the problem are parents. They have the ability to recognize and meet the instances of anger in their children. They have the opportunity to bring positive, teachable moments out of these situations.

But in many or most cases, that is not happening. Parents simply lack the understanding of how to deal with their children's emotions, and kids are learning to handle their emotions inappropriately and immaturely. They will in turn pass these misunderstandings on to their children, who will one day become parents and perpetuate the same errors. The Old Testament tells us that the sins of the fathers are often visited upon several generations of their children, and it's not difficult to see why. We are the only parenting and life management models our children have.

At the very center of the problem is the issue of power. When children first come into this world, they soon discover that they lack power, and they seek any possible way of controlling their world. As they grow older, autonomy becomes a significant goal— they long to feel and appear proudly independent. Taken by itself, this desire for control and for personal autonomy is not a bad thing. But these things must be sensitively and wisely granted, based on specific levels of growth and maturity. It is not appropriate to grant a two-year-old child the freedom to cross a busy street, though the child may cry out for this right. It is not appropriate for a preadolescent to roam the Internet without supervision, though she may balk at restrictions. How will you handle the anger that arises from everyday discipline?

Your consistent goal is for your children to learn respect for other people and particularly for authority. Achieving that goal will mean that children learn how to handle inevitable conflict: first over a toy, later over a playground dispute, then someday over complex adult social transactions. Poor control of anger is a national epidemic, and your children's only hope lies in proper parenting on your part. The way you handle anger today will powerfully influence the way they handle anger tomorrow. They certainly cannot hope to see effective models of anger management at work in the world that we have experienced.

Another consistent goal for your children is that they become people of integrity. This word comes not only from the idea of honesty, but from the concept of being whole and complete—living lives of consistency, which means acting with the same character qualities in one situation as in another.

I've written this book so that your children might have a better opportunity to become strong individuals and good citizens, respectful of authority and grounded in a pure and consistent character. Here's a compelling definition of integrity that every parent should inscribe upon the hearts of children. Review it again and again; discuss it; model it; honor it.

People of integrity:
- Tell the truth,
- Keep promises,
- Take responsibility for their actions.

Poor management of anger is associated with low integrity and an antiauthority sensibility. People with mishandled anger will resent authority, and they will be driven to lie, to break promises, and to behave poorly on a regular basis. I have never met a parent who wishes to raise a child with low integrity and a rebellious spirit, one driven daily by anger and resentment. We all want better for our children, and we need help dealing with the central emotional issues.

The Priority of Love

Where does all this anger originate? We work hard to give our children happy homes. Why are they angry, and why are they likely to become angry adults?

The difficult truth is that the greatest source of anger in children is a deep-rooted belief that they are not loved. Children instinctively realize they need love and that their parents are responsible to give it to them. While young children may be incapable of expressing such a complex idea, they know they cannot live happily or develop normally without the security that comes from unconditional love.

We must face the fact that very few children feel this love from their parents in a genuine and absolute sense. And when they feel deep in their hearts that Mom and Dad have withheld this gift of love, the natural response will always be anger. Certainly there are other causes of childhood anger or rage, usually specific events such as disappointments, conflicts, abuse, fears, losses, and so on. But the greatest of these is not feeling loved. Even in the best of homes, too many children crave love desperately, even as their parents believe the need has been met.

Perhaps you're very troubled by what you're reading, and you're offended by the very idea that your children do not feel loved. Very few parents who participate in my workshops immediately acknowledge that their own children would fall into this category. Let's look a little deeper at why this problem could be present—even in your home.

I believe most parents truly love their children. The problem comes in their ability to transmit their heartfelt love to the heart of the child. The message is not coming through.

Still you might object. You might assure me: "I tell my daughter I love her every single day!" And you would be telling the truth. The fact is that most parents are verbal in their basic orientation. Therefore, they assume that telling a child, "I love you," settles the issue.

The verbal expression of love is important indeed, but it's far from sufficient. While we as parents are verbal creatures, our children are behavioral. And to communicate with anyone, we must speak the person's language. If you want to give a clear and precise message to someone who speaks French, then you must learn the nuances of speaking the French language. If you want to communicate with your child in the most profound and effective way, you must do so not on your terms but on your child's, and those terms are behavioral ones. We will deal with this idea more thoroughly in subsequent chapters, and you can also learn more about this subject in my two previous books, *How to Really Love Your Child* and *How to Really Love Your Teenager*. For the time being, let me underline this point for you: if your children do not feel loved, they cannot grow to be the best persons they are capable of becoming. They will carry within them a sense of this failure, and they will feel continuing anger toward their parents. This anger interferes with a child's basic development and later with adult behavior.

Here is a tangible illustration of the difference between verbal and behavioral communication. Years ago, when I was traveling, I could call home and say to my wife, "I just wanted to tell you that I love you." That was all she needed to hear; the words were a warm affirmation for her.

Then she might have handed the phone to Dale, my five-year-old son. I would repeat the words, telling him I loved him. "Sure," he was likely to respond. "But, Daddy, why did you call?"

The verbal expression of love was meaningful and nurturing to my verbally oriented wife, but the same expression didn't carry much significance for Dale. Being a child, he was behavioral in nature. To convey the message of love from my heart to his meant acting out my love when I returned home. I might pick him up and give him a great hug, and I might bring him a gift. I might sit down with him and take a close look at the play activities in which he was engaged. I might play ball with him in the front yard. These actions on my part would give him the same message my wife received when I simply said, "I love you."

Angry and Helpless

In his book *Make Anger Your Ally*, Neil Clark Warren offers some perceptive definitions of anger and explanations of its various causes. For our purposes, we can apply his ideas specifically to the world of children.

The capacity to become angry is an impressive gift which comes as part of our biological inheritance.

Anger is a physical state of readiness. When we are angry, we are prepared to act. ...

The whole purpose of anger is to give us the wherewithal for managing our environment—particularly those parts which cause us to feel hurt, frustrated, or fearful. If we do that poorly, we will regularly experience a sense of inadequacy and helplessness.[1]

By all means, think about yourself as you read these words. Think about your anger and how it relates to the world around you. Then think about your children. Reflect on the things that make them angry and how they express that anger. Think, too, about children in good homes where certain events and emotions transcend their capacity to understand or interpret their feelings correctly.

Dr. Warren makes another observation worthy of examination. He asserts that the single most important factor in handling anger is a person's self-concept. He writes that a "solidly constructed self-system" is the key to taking charge of one's life. An abundant supply of self-esteem provides the energy we need to make life satisfying and fruitful.[2] Then, working from this healthy foundation, we have a base for personal power and autonomy. We are less prone to insecurity and thus slower to anger. Power flows from positive self-concept.

What about children? They, too, become angry when a situation or a person seems frustrating, threatening, or hurtful. The problem is that, unlike adults, children lack the power to make radical changes in their lives. They have a weak power base, little autonomy, and only occasional and very limited independence.

Consider also that unlike most adults, children have no firmly established self-system in place. Ideally, parents or other adults are helping them to form a self-concept. Some kids may even possess a remarkably well-formed self-concept for their age. What they lack, however, is a clear comprehension of the world around them—the world of parents, the community, the school, and their friends. They have not accumulated sufficient experience to enable them to interpret the world in relation to themselves. And knowledge is power; children feel this lack of power.

Parents serve as guides down the long, winding path of character formation. All along the way, children plant delicate seeds of integrity, creativity, self-esteem, love, industry, and many other qualities. We must tread gently on this journey. To deliberately frustrate these children, or to "cause one of these little ones to stumble" (as Jesus put it), is a bit like putting on hiking boots and trampling through the beautiful flowers they have carefully cultivated.

But these are more than flowers that are being nurtured; we are dealing with human souls of God's creation and special intentions, with eternal consequences. Perhaps this is why Jesus said, "It would be better for [the hurtful adult] to be thrown into the sea with a millstone tied around his neck than for him to cause one of these little ones to sin. So watch yourselves," (Luke 17:2-3). Children are wonderful creations of God with incredible potential. It's a grave responsibility to serve as their guides in the journey of learning to manage life.

This is a sobering issue that deserves your serious consideration. Could it be possible that you are unintentionally causing young ones to stumble? What are the practical dynamics within your family relationships? How do you handle conversation at the dinner table? In family meetings? How do you respond when your child brings you some request? Some problem? How do you handle a failure? Have you ever placed yourself in the shoes of your child and reflected upon how you might respond in these situations? If your child seems regularly frustrated, is there something in your behavior that exacerbates the problem?

Every family has regular episodes of crisis and confrontation, but what you say—as well as how you say it—is crucial.

The Many Shapes and Colors of Anger

Let's move back to the personal perspective for a moment. Imagine yourself in a threatening situation. Perhaps you have just discovered that your job is in jeopardy. Or perhaps that car behind you on the interstate has been tailgating you for the last five miles. How will you express your frustration?

We express our anger, in the words of Neil Clark Warren, to "manage those internal and external sources of hurt, frustration, and threat" and keep "inner pain to an absolute minimum."[3] Think of the tea kettle. When the pressure and heat build up inside, there has to be an outlet. The whistle is useful, for it lets us know the water has reached a certain level of temperature. In the same way, your anger symptoms let others know the level of pressure building up inside you.

There are few differences in the ways children and adults express anger. Yes, adults use a larger vocabulary and have a wider variety of resources to draw from—including physical strength. But when some adult in close proximity to you loses his temper, you can squint your eyes and nearly convince yourself that you are watching an eight-year-old. Old habits die hard, even those of emotional expression.

On the other hand, adults are working from a power base when they express their anger. Therein lies the difference. Children "act out" from a dependent state, as well as from their immature understandings of the world around them. They may be clever enough when it comes to using leverage and manipulation, but there is rarely power enough to effect the changes they desire. If you have an impulse to buy the overly expensive new dress or the golf bag in the shop window, you at least possess the means and ability to walk into the store and purchase the item or not. The little girl who sees the fabulous dollhouse has no power at all, no voice in the matter. She has no power base and also lacks the understanding of why such a wonderful purchase might be an inappropriate one.

In most cases, you can identify the source of your distress and even how it might ideally be resolved. This isn't always true for a child—she knows when she is angry because she can't have the dollhouse, but she cannot identify the more complex issues in her environment that upset her. Therefore, you constantly need to ask, "What is bothering this child? What does she want? Is it something appropriate? Did someone else cause the distress or frustration?"

Children may well have desires that are neither reasonable nor realistic. They may just wish they were older or bigger, or had more power or space or money. They may be responding to growth cycles or hormones. They may have been treated unfairly by people whose actions even parents cannot control. They may envy the possessions or privileges of friends.

But there are also times when you will recognize the source of the hurt or frustration, and it will be possible for you to make amends. You might even be the cause of the frustration. Take every measure and make every effort to make things right. Growing up is hard enough without people we love making it more difficult.

Looking Ahead

Perhaps you've spent many hours dreaming about your children's future. You envision them living healthy and productive lives, excelling in their careers and producing adorable grandchildren. Naturally you haven't spent any time at all considering what bitter fruit anger may bring about in their lives. It isn't the kind of thing that makes for pleasant daydreams. Yet the greatest and most pervasive threat to a healthy and happy life for your child is the presence of unacknowledged and mishandled anger. Its damage extends to mind, soul, spirit, and strength. We can trace virtually every problem of adult life back to that one common source.

Indeed, we have seen that bitter fruit. We live in a world of road rage, domestic violence, adolescent suicide, rising terrorism, anger-driven politics, hate groups, shock radio, and countless other symptoms of a very angry world. As the prophet Isaiah described it, "Oh, the raging of many nations—they rage like the raging sea," (Isa. 17:12). We owe it to our children and the future of our society to recognize and deal with the root problems now, while our kids are young and teachable and before the damage is done.

But our efforts must begin with the reflection we see in the mirror. We cannot teach our children until we ourselves have taken in the lessons and been transformed by them. That means learning to handle our own anger. In chapter 8, we will take a close look at what parents need to understand in order to be able to train their children.

I am a fortunate father. When my children were young, I had no idea how to help them handle their anger. But I learned these vital lessons just in time—early enough that my wife and I could train our children when they were small. Our goal was to have them reach a significant level of maturity by the time they were 17, so that both we and they could feel confident of their passage into the adult world.

Carey, David, and Dale are now adults who manage their anger and their lives well—sometimes, to my surprise and amusement, much better than I do. As I observe them, one of my greatest joys in life is to see them functioning as young adults of integrity and strong character.

I am also profoundly thankful that my children are free of the typical emotional scars and pain that so many children carry into adult life. I refer especially to that sense of deprivation, that nagging sense that something vital is missing from their lives. This feeling prevents many adults from being and doing all that they

would like to be and do. It comes not only from a lack of unconditional love, but also from the mishandling of anger.

Two of the greatest gifts you can give your children are to love
them unconditionally and to teach them to manage their anger in
ever more mature ways. Our goals with this book, then, are ambi-
tious; let us begin the journey.

2

An Atmosphere of Anger

*Just a few decades ago, a child might have been born into a com-*munity filled with love and nurturing. An unspoken assumption was that the innocence of children was something sacred and precious, a thing to be protected at great cost.

In those days, society was child-friendly in many ways. People took it for granted that children were special, to be cherished and loved. Those who felt otherwise were considered to be missing something essential to the normal human experience. Yes, it was sometimes said that "children should be seen, not heard," but then again, there were scrupulous limitations to what children themselves could see and hear. Even television, dubbed from the beginning a "vast wasteland" of culture, recognized tremendous self-restraint. Evening was a time for family programming, and a great many of the shows were light-hearted depictions of healthy families.

These conditions prevailed for various reasons, but among those reasons was the central value of childhood as a nation's treasure, and innocence as the defining quality of youth. The feeling, expressed so beautifully by the psalmist, was that children "are a heritage from the LORD … a reward from him. Like arrows in the hands of a warrior are sons born in one's youth. Blessed is the man whose quiver is full of them" (Ps. 127:3–5). Adults often saw this as a reason for living: firing those arrows of offspring into a future they would not themselves live to see. To this end, families were built around molding healthy, happy children into wise, effective adults.

But over the past several decades, an ominous change has come over our cultural world. Not only are children exposed to shocking language and ideas at nearly every turn and in every form of media expression, but sometimes it seems that the world no longer likes children very much. More and more, children are referred to and depicted as inherently annoying, hindrances to adult freedom. They do not express the purpose of family but are merely a "lifestyle option." Childless couples generally are depicted as free and fun-loving, heading for the ski slopes on a whim, or onto the cruise ship for a spontaneous voyage to the Bahamas. Children, according to some, "tie us down."

Those who do become parents often are encouraged to pursue their own personal fulfillment first and to seek plenty of "personal space" to limit the hindrance of living with children and their endless needs. And as we all know, more children than ever are ignored; more than ever are abused; more than ever are acting out their confusion in violent or inappropriate ways.

We must ask the question: Do we still love children—not just our own but the whole idea of them? Do we consider childhood to be sacred and inviolable? The hard facts would suggest an answer we may not be eager to acknowledge.

Kids in the Town Square

Children's needs generally receive a low financial priority in the public realm. Even hardened criminals receive better services than many of our children. Public officials are well aware of the needs of children, but when they run for office, they seem to feel that there are other "hot buttons" that will gather votes more quickly. We are more concerned about taxes, about crime, or about the environment or some other issue.

Meanwhile, a growing sea of data suggests that public education is moving in the wrong direction. The enduring images of our schools are pictures of chaos, of children with guns, and of high school graduates who cannot read but are recruited by major universities to play football. The Centers for Disease Control in Atlanta have listed school violence as a public health concern in the United States. We have seen a growing epidemic of bullying taken to a level that is dangerous both physically and emotionally.

Meanwhile, the entertainment industry no longer sees itself as having a duty to protect children. On the contrary, it seems engaged in a war against teenagers and children, sending them spiritual poison in the forms of sex, violence, and degenerate values. Kids are specifically targeted by some of the worst motion pictures, TV shows, Web sites, and video games. Advertisers exploit the weaknesses and desires of the young.

As crime has busted out of our control, the victims have more than ever been children. Criminals are devious enough to prey upon teenage runaways, quickly getting them addicted to drugs and involved in child pornography. Am I resorting to overblown sensationalism? Hardly. If you live in the city, ask your local police. They will tell you that purveyors of drugs and pornography are systematic and businesslike in the way they recruit and exploit young victims.

Then there is the issue of responsibility. Who is ever at fault? We see this phenomenon played out over and over; someone is caught in wrongdoing and points the finger elsewhere—at parents, authority, or society itself. We have become a nation of victims. This scapegoat mentality, too, victimizes the young, because our children pick up the idea that there is no accountability. Blame can be shifted elsewhere, like pushing old toys under the bed rather than cleaning the room.

Childhood is harsher, but it is also shorter than it used to be. Kids grow up all too quickly today, finding themselves launched at the preadolescent stage into an aggressive, permissive adult world. We are less likely to look at children as our reason and responsibility for living, our hope for the future, and the greatest joy of our hearts—and more likely to look upon them as young consumers, a target for profit rather than a source for joy.

Perhaps you are one of those parents who has seen all these developments and bridled with frustration. What can be done? How can an evil culture be brought back into control? What difference can one parent, or even a group of parents, make? Those with Judeo-Christian values no longer seem to call the shots. Whether we are still a swelling majority or an ebbing minority, we are surely downtrodden and discouraged. We only know that we love our own children, and we will do whatever is possible to protect them from a cynical, self-destructive world. We will teach them all that we know about the values that should still be lived out. As an article in Reader's Digest said, "The barbarians are not at the gates. They are inside. The question of the hour—and of the next century—is whether all this can be turned around."[1]

An old cartoon showed a huge crowd; every person in the crowd bore a perplexed expression and a thought balloon. Every single character was thinking, "But what can one person do?" Each one was brooding on the same thought privately while standing in a sea of individuals who felt the same way. The best hope for the future of our children is for a sea of frustrated, perplexed parents to look around and discover one another and to say, "One of us may be fairly helpless, but together we are an army—and we are ready to take action!"

Looking for Love

Children receive love and the nurturing of a sense of personal identity from three sources. In these places, they find out who they are and how they are to think about life:

• Home and family. The family is the immediate circle of nurturers, as well as a world of aunts, uncles, grandparents, and anyone who cares deeply about the child.

• Community. This has many manifestations: the all-important school, the clubs and social organizations, athletic teams, and the other ways we organize ourselves locally.

• Church. This is a place for children to learn of God's love for them and to discover a unique and special identity in the context of what the New Testament calls "the body of Christ." Support, fellowship, and usefulness are found here.

Most of us would agree on the primacy of these three basic centers for character formation. Yet stop and consider the children of today's world. The majority of them have little or no church affiliation. Communities are fractured in an increasingly urbanized and segmented society. And what about family, the essential and irreplaceable unit? More families than ever are troubled and broken.

At the end of the day, then, we realize that children are quite fortunate to be getting their "minimum social requirements" from one to two of the three categories above. A child growing in the context of a strong family, community, and church has a tremendous advantage—but he or she is the exception rather than the rule today. Instead, we have a world where children often fend for themselves as adults pursue their busy schedules. This is an economically rich generation of children in comparative terms, but a flood of toys and games won't provide them with their most essential personal needs: unconditional love and a satisfying sense of identity.

The Great Rebellion

Imagine Joey, an ordinary little boy. Joey's parents love him, but Dad is preoccupied with work, and Mom is preoccupied with many other pursuits. Neither is particularly affectionate by nature. For many complex reasons, they fail to give Joey the love he needs and craves. They also fail to realize what is lacking. Deep within Joey, the anger begins to build and to deepen. In a short period of time, the anger of love deficiency begins to take the outward form of rebellion—rebellion against parents, against teachers, against other children and their parents. Rebellion always finds its ultimate expression in an antiauthority disposition. As Joey grows older, he begins to attack and undermine authority figures wherever they appear. His parents recognize the anger, and they're puzzled by it. They don't know how to teach him to handle his emotions appropriately. This pattern will play out destructively and self-destructively throughout Joey's life unless it is recognized, confronted, and healed.

We see antiauthority attitudes all around us in the adult world. If you stop and think about your own social world, you'll realize that many of your friends and family have tendencies toward rebelling against bosses, pastors, or other forms of authorities. We see the bumper sticker that says, "Question Authority." It represents a common modern sentiment, for there may never have been a time as deeply rebellious as the one in which we live. A generation of children has needed love, and it has then needed to know what to do with the heat of its emotions.

Let us say it again: Our widespread rebellion against authority springs from anger.

Anger springs from being inadequately loved.

And the lack of love in childhood is an issue for parents.

Many years ago, people were discussing and debating Robert Nisbet's book, *The Decline of Authority*. The problem seemed theoretical and academic—not an issue of everyday living. But as the years have gone by, Nisbet's work has taken on the status of prophecy fulfilled. We don't see a mere tendency toward rebellion; we see an entire social fabric so entrenched in striking out against authority that we take it all for granted.

Dr. Benjamin Spock, the legendary specialist in children's medicine, despaired over this social fabric before his death in 1998. In his book *A Better World for Our Children*, he wrote of his deep mourning over the "brutal state of our neighborhoods, where our children now dodge bullets instead of playing dodge ball," and where children must deal with divorce and violence in their daily lives. Dr. Spock pointed to a fundamental loss of values as the cause of this deterioration.[2]

Morality in this country has reached an all-time low in the last 25 years—especially in the last 10 years. In this short span, we have heard educators tell teens that their bodies are their own and that they can do with them what they want, including any kind of sexual activity or abortion.

The language and actions common in "family entertainment" used to be prohibited on stage and screen.

And crime? In the era of the O. J. Simpson trial, we have come to expect a "crime scandal of the day," even among movie stars, athletes, and government figures. Murders and robberies that may have made headlines half a century ago are now too ordinary to make the news.

Even in our churches, we see the influence of social rebellion. People are rejecting the authority figures of religion and tradition in favor of individualized faith expressions where the worshiper makes the decisions about what kinds of music to hear, what sermon content is "relevant," and of course, "my own interpretation of the Bible." If I can interpret the Scriptures however they become most convenient, I become the only authority in faith issues—and this is well in keeping with the temperament of our times, when we resent anyone telling us what to do or think. Inevitably, of course, we cannot escape conflict. Churches today are filled with disputes and controversies as laymen and women refuse to submit to one another in love in the way the New Testament pleads with us to do.

It is a world of rebellion and anger, and peace becomes an impossible dream.

Taking Responsibility

We no longer trust public leaders, and the reason is more than our own rebellious attitudes. The leaders themselves have largely abandoned the idea of accountability. They, too, often feel no responsibility to keep campaign pledges. They fail to honor the public trust. In this of all areas in which we should be able to expect models of integrity, we take it for granted that honesty is in short supply. Over and over we have seen the spectacle of cornered politicians, caught in compromising acts, who cannot simply say, "I was wrong. I apologize. The buck stops here, and I take full responsibility."

Taking responsibility means facing the fact that we may be wrong, in opinion or behavior. It means constantly evaluating our behavior and being willing to correct it when we need to. If we fail to do this, we find ourselves blaming others.

A few years back, a dentist unhappily found himself in the daily news. He had molested some of his female patients and therefore lost his license. His response was to sue his insurance company for disability pay to the tune of a million dollars. How did he justify this? He claimed that his behavior resulted from "mental illness," a recent phenomenon we all recognize: calling any kind of inappropriate behavior a "condition" or "illness." That way, the adultery, the embezzlement, the physical abuse, or the dereliction of duty is not one's own fault; it's simply an "illness" or some new social problem. This helps people dodge accountability.

We need a return to the quality of integrity expressed by General Eisenhower during World War II. Before the invasion, he prepared a press release to be made public in the event of a failed mission. The release read, in part, "If any blame or fault attaches to the attempt, it is mine alone." We now consider such personal responsibility the uncommon act of a hero, but in the past it was merely expected.

Signs of Hope

We tend to forget that there are indeed appropriate methods of expressing anger. The shining example of well-handled anger is the organization known as Mothers Against Drunk Driving (MADD). In 1980, a group of grieving mothers came together and decided to channel their grief into something that would touch the future in a positive way. They began their organization with its first chapters in California and Maryland. Since that time, alcohol-related traffic fatalities have declined by an amazing 43 percent—and much of that decline can surely be attributed to the effective and persistent work of MADD.

Those mothers were angry not just at the particular drivers whose intoxication had taken away their children's lives; they were angry at a society that tolerated the terrible phenomenon of drunken driving. They applied the energy of their emotions in the place where the most good could be done. And today we even have SADD—Students Against Drunk Driving. The movement has spread to the impressionable younger people who are in the best position to stop the madness.

How about the deep anger brought about by racial issues? Martin Luther King's peaceful marches against discrimination are another brilliant example of taking anger and making something good from it. Dr. King instructed his followers to demonstrate peacefully, then cooperate when they were arrested and jailed. The integrity of this approach did more to spur on the Civil Rights Movement than violent anger might have ever done.

In 1982, Deborah Larbalestrier, an older woman living in Los Angeles, became a household name on the West Coast because of her courageous use of her anger. Living in a crime-ridden section of the city, she felt helpless to stop what was happening all around her. But then one day she saw two boys trying to steal her neighbor's car. They knew she was watching, and the whole scene outraged her. The Los Angeles Times reported what happened next:

> I went out there with a stick and I told them, "How dare you insult me that way, robbing this car right in my face as if I didn't exist?"
> The teenagers ran off, but Larbalestrier wanted to make sure they didn't return. So she called a meeting on her block and told them, "We've become prisoners in our own homes. … We have to take our neighborhood back."
> Then Larbalestrier went to the Los Angeles Police Department's Wilshire Division to organize a Neighborhood Watch club for her street.[3]

By the time the article was written, the neighborhood had been crime-free for 18 months. Appropriate ways to handle anger can be profoundly redemptive.

Children and Hope for Society

Every society reflects what its children know: Yesterday's children are today's adults, and the children in your home will soon be grown. There is hope for our society if enough people learn how to use their anger appropriately and constructively. Anger does not have to lead to violence. It need never rage out of control. Anger, we too often forget, is not in itself a sin—the Bible teaches us that sin arises out of how we use our anger. If we can only see it and approach it in a new way, this painful emotion can become a gift to be used to make the world—and our own lives—stronger and more peaceful.

There is hope for society if parents will become more intentional about teaching their children how to manage anger. For many parents, this will first mean learning to understand and manage their own anger in better ways.

It will also include teaching children to respect authority, regardless of whether they happen to agree with the stance of that authority. Again, parents themselves must first come to terms with their own rebellious attitudes. Children watch and learn. They might hear you expressing your contempt for the leaders of your church, and they come to share that contempt. Or instead, they might hear you talking about ways to help those same leaders do a better job. Perhaps without even realizing it, you will have taught your children a lesson in the appropriate uses of anger.

Even when you are satisfied that your children are dealing with their own anger appropriately, you will always have to remain aware that the world is filled with other children and adults who are not. At least one-third of adolescents are subjected to abusive relationships. Children are committing unprecedented cruelty and violence. Teenagers make up only 7 percent of the population, yet they commit 17 percent of violent crimes.

You envision a much better world for your children—not a world characterized by anger and rebellion, but one in which they follow your lead as models of unquestioned integrity; a world they can improve by reaching out to others and helping them handle anger the right way. The problem is massive and causes us to despair. But there is hope if we join hands. What can one person do? We can assemble the people we love, as Deborah Larbalestrier did. We can say, "This has gone far enough. We need to take back our neighborhoods. We need to take back our churches. We need to take back our schools and our workplaces and make them places of peace and not violence. Yes, we are angry, but we will beat our swords into plowshares. We will till the social soil around us until its harvest is one of peace."

3

A House on Fire

Close your eyes and visualize this wonderful scene.

The front doorbell rings. You open the door to find a man dressed in overalls and holding some kind of equipment. He looks like the kind of worker who might come to spray for bugs. Instead, he smiles politely and says, "I'm the Anger Exterminator, and I'm here to treat your home."

You step aside and let the man walk into your front hallway. He heads down the hallway and enters your first grader's bedroom. "Hi, little fellow," he says, and there's a pause as he seems to be checking for something. Then you hear a "whisk, whisk" sound as he sprays something in the room. Your nose can already pick up the pleasant, sweet smell.

Then you hear the footsteps heading into your teenager's room. "Anger Exterminator, young lady," he says politely. Just like always, your daughter begins loudly protesting. But you hear and smell the spray-can once again. The exterminator hesitates. "Uh oh," he says. "You've got a pretty considerable anger buildup here—worse than last week. Tough day at school, eh? These clouds are pretty dark ones." Your daughter again protests, but not as vehemently. That spray is already working.

Clump, clump, clump! The man hauls his heavy equipment back downstairs and says, "Now I need to spray you and your spouse, if you please."

"Oh, but we're not angry," you smile.

"Just a few little friendly disagreements, you know … " your spouse says quickly.

"Gotta do my job," the man grins. "You have more anger clouds floating around here than you realize. If you let those things get into the air, you'll be choking before you know it."

Whisk! Whisk, whisk! The spray feels cool, and you have to admit that you feel lighter and fresher than you did a few moments ago. You had forgotten how bright and cheerful the room looked without those clouds.

"See you next month," you smile as the man climbs back into his truck. And for the next few days, your house has that clean and pleasant aroma—lots of laughter and kidding, very few arguments. You had become accustomed to the dark clouds, but their absence is wonderful.

Wouldn't it be nice if technology could provide us such a thing as an "anger exterminator"? What if you had a special mat outside your door, and you could wipe off all the unpleasant problems and conflicts—just like mud—rather than track them into your clean home?

How we would love it if anger actually came in clouds or clumps, and we could be rid of its clutches so simply. How fresh and pleasant our homes would be. But as we all know, anger is more like a disease that infects those who come into contact with it. We are all, as members of the human race, carriers of this disease. We are exposed wherever we go, picking up the deadly bacteria of anger and carrying it into our homes, where we pass it on to one another.

It may not come in clouds, and it may not come in clumps. But at least anger is not an incurable disease. There are ways to recognize it, meet it, handle it, and keep our homes as clean and free as possible from the deadly tentacles of seething anger.

Keeping the Air Clean

Tropical fish hobbyists know that an aquarium needs a certain amount of maintenance. An aquarium needs a working filter and, from time to time, a thorough cleaning of the tank. How much more maintenance, then, is required for a clean and healthy home for human children? The atmosphere of the home has a tremendous effect on the spirit and self-concept of any child.

When I enter a home, I can quickly tell whether a child will thrive there. Each home has its own unique atmosphere. Some of its qualities are fairly neutral, like colors and styles, while other traits tend to be more positive or negative.

The atmosphere in one home may be warm, relaxed, calm, friendly, accepting, and upbeat. People feel comfortable in such a home, and children living there can grow to be their best. They can relax in the support and encouragement that the parents provide; they can use their energies to develop in every part of their lives.

However, precious few family groups meet that ideal. Far too many children live in homes filled with some combination of tension, judgment, pessimism, and rejection. Children have to expend most of their energy simply trying to cope with the lack of love and support. Because it's more difficult for them to develop normally in this atmosphere, children will increasingly feel anger toward their parents. They will be denied the love they need, and the guidance they need in dealing with the resulting anger.

Here is the key insight: You, the parent, determine the atmosphere of your home. You set the pace. You build the foundation of love and acceptance. You are the trainer in anger management. Many parents speak as if their power as parents is limited and they're already doing all they can. But in truth, we have a great deal of power and our children have almost none.

Naturally, you want to feel good about your parenting performance. We all do. After all, these are our lives, our homes, our families—the major investment of all that we have in time, money, and emotion. We want that investment to bring wonderful dividends not simply in our peace of mind, but in happy and productive children who will make us proud and joyful. As new parents, of course, we have few doubts. It's easy to envision our toddlers as future presidents, Super Bowl quarterbacks, and discoverers of the cure for cancer. Our babies are tiny, dependent, and fully within our control.

But as time passes and children grow older and more independent, we may give in to discouragement. It's not so easy after all to mold a wise, self-actualized, and happy human being. We see the anger flare up from nowhere like a sudden thunderstorm, and we are puzzled and frustrated. Where did this outburst come from? Where have we gone wrong as parents? What became of that happy toddler? We begin to wonder in the back of our minds if we have failed at the greatest and central purpose life has given us—and the idea of failure in that area is unthinkable. No wonder we begin to build our own levels of anger. We feel we have given our kids all we have to give, and here they are striking out at us.

Those manifestations of anger can be horrifying. Consider the stories of Ann and Todd.

The Story of Ann

The couple made a nice picture as they entered the door of my office. They were attractive, cordial, and well-dressed. Their names were Jim and Mary Perkins, and my appointment book filled in the background: they had a 15-year-old daughter named Ann.

Ann was finishing her first trimester of pregnancy.

Mary, Ann's mother, had a familiar face. "I'm certain we've met before," I smiled.

"I've shown you to a table at the Sailmaker," she said. The Sailmaker was a local restaurant.

"Of course. You're the hostess at lunchtime. I was there just last Tuesday."

I turned to Jim and asked about his work. He told me he was an accountant.

"That figures," I grinned, using a very old and very stale pun— just something to break the ice. The Perkinses chuckled a bit nervously. We made a bit more small talk and discovered we had mutual friends from their church. Finally, I glanced at my appointment book and came to business. "You came to talk about Ann," I said to Mary. "Why not tell me about her?"

Mary's tears welled up almost instantly. "Dr. Campbell, she's only 15, just a year out of middle school. The youngest of our four—and she's gotten herself pregnant! What are we going to do?"

The words and the tears flooded out as if the dam had finally burst. "We did everything we knew how to do as parents," said Mary. "We worked long hours—both of us—to give our kids the good things in life. We took them to church and Scouts and piano lessons and music camp. You name it, we found a way to give it to them. Ann is so talented, so beautiful. What are we going to do?" And Mary's voice trailed off in despair as she repeated that refrain.

Jim twisted in his chair. Where his wife had painted a portrait in sorrow, her husband's medium was disgust. "How could she get herself into this mess?" he snarled. "She strikes out at us every chance she gets. She argues with everything we say. Where does all that pure defiance come from?"

I listened carefully to Mary and Jim and drew two conclusions:

1. They loved their daughter very much.
2. They attempted to express that love through gifts and advantages.

I'm not certain they had seen the situation exactly that way, but they clearly believed they should exchange time with Ann for things for Ann.

When I met with the teenager herself, my suspicions were confirmed. From her vantage point, it wasn't clear at all that her parents loved her. She didn't even feel she was a particularly important factor in their lives. She said carelessly, "I don't know why I got pregnant. I just did. I could easily have prevented it." Ann paused and looked at me closely. "Maybe I wanted to be somebody, too, like my mother," she said quietly. "If I became a mother, then I would be important, wouldn't I? Then maybe someone would love me."

Pain and Healing

I led a number of sessions with Ann and her parents together. In our first hours, the girl was reserved and expressed few feelings, though her anger and frustration were clear enough. After several sessions, she began to share more candidly.

"Remember the night of the mother-daughter banquet, Mom? You couldn't be there because you had to go with Daddy to his business social. I was the only one at the banquet without a mother."

"But, Ann," Mary interrupted, "we talked about that—don't you remember? I bought you a lovely dress for the banquet. I thought you were coming out ahead, and you were OK with it. You didn't seem to mind that I went with Daddy."

"Well, I did mind! You guys never seem to be around when I need you. My friends' parents always drive us to games and stuff; you never offer to drive. I'm always bumming rides with someone else."

Her father jumped into the fray. "Now wait a minute, Ann," he argued. "You speak as if we never do anything for you. You are quite an accomplished pianist. Who took you to all those lessons? Who paid for them? Doesn't that mean anything to you?"

Ann shrugged. "Not much, Daddy. Anyway, how would you know whether I can play the piano? The last time you attended one of my recitals was when I was ten."

These emotional confrontations came frequently, and I noticed that Jim usually rose from his chair and left the room when he saw an outburst coming. He couldn't stand the pain of confrontation.

And yet there was progress. I sensed that, for the first time, Jim and Mary were beginning to understand how Ann felt about things. They realized for the first time that their daughter valued their time and attention more than their gifts and privileges. Ann had plenty of possessions and camp trips, but her well of emotional fulfillment was dry. She was thirsty for their love and nurture. Jim and Mary had simply never seen her in that light.

To their credit, the two parents redoubled their efforts to understand Ann's world and her problems. They looked for new ways to be a part of her life, to share her joys and sorrows. For her part, Ann began to realize her parents actually loved her more than she had assumed; they simply hadn't known how to show it. And she began to reach out to them, to communicate more clearly how she felt and what she needed.

It was a slow and painful process, but Ann and her parents began to really get acquainted with each other as if they had been strangers for years. Because all three of them deeply desired a loving family—and were willing to work to repair the damage and make a fresh start—success was possible. Ann began to experience the love she had always craved, and her anger began to subside.

There were still problems, still scars. A baby was still on the way. But as three hurting people clung to each other and became a true family unit, their love covered a multitude of past sins—and the future requirements of hard times.

The Story of Todd

The Johnsons, like the Perkinses, made an impressive appearance; they also made an impatient one. Mark Johnson sat across the room, restlessly tapping his well-manicured fingers on the arm of the chair. He was clearly a man ill-accustomed to being at the mercy of someone else's schedule. His well-dressed wife, Brenda, was equally impatient.

The Johnsons were active members of a large church. They were prominent in the community, well-liked, and affluent. They had two children: Todd, eleven, and Amy, six. I had gathered this much information prior to our appointment, but I had yet to learn why they wanted to meet with me.

Brenda Johnson began, "Dr. Campbell, it's about our son, Todd. Since he was very little, Todd was always happy and healthy and normal. But in the last six months, some kind of change has come over him. Now we seem to have a quiet stranger in our home, one who is angry nearly all the time. We try to spend time with him, which can be quite a sacrifice when we hardly have time for each other. But Todd avoids us with every kind of excuse. My husband has a growing law practice, and I operate a children's clothing store. So, yes, we stay busy, but we're trying unsuccessfully to attend to our son and his problems."

Mark Johnson added, "Our daughter is living proof we're not such bad parents. She appreciates everything we do for her. Amy knows her parents put in long hours to give her a comfortable home, and she hasn't given us any trouble. Why Todd is so different, I haven't a clue." Mark cleared his throat and exchanged a cautious glance with his wife. It was clear we were about to get down to business. "Dr. Campbell, a few nights ago, Todd was driven home by some of his older friends. He was completely drunk. Eleven years old and drunk! What in the world could have gotten into a boy from a fine, hard-working, church-going family?"

We all sat silently for a moment, then Brenda took up the story. "Our son has disrupted the household with his little stunt, and that is not acceptable. Mark had to reschedule some very important appointments in his practice, and I'm missing time and revenue at my shop. Don't misunderstand us, Dr. Campbell; we love our son, and we want to help him; we want to help ourselves. But it makes no sense at all. Why is he doing this to us? Why would he repay all our love and sacrifice with pain and anger?"

"I'm one of the best lawyers in town," said Mark, who was now pacing my office floor. "I can resolve all kinds of convoluted legal problems, but I can't solve an 11-year-old's problems."

Todd, as we discovered, had already accumulated more experience with alcohol than his parents had realized. And he wasn't alone. Studies show that an increasing number of young teens and preteens are using alcohol and drugs. Many of these are from fine, conservative Christian families. It's certainly one way of getting their parents' complete attention.

Todd's family life had been deteriorating, as spotless and proper as his parents perceived it to be. The focus was on career and earning, not on love and nurturing. Todd felt unloved and angry about it, and that made him a target for falling into the wrong crowd. Misery loves company, and angry kids gravitate toward groups of other angry kids. All he had to do to find attention and acceptance in a peer group was to do what they pressured him to do. This particular group nudged him into alcohol abuse, but it might also have been sexual misbehavior, theft, vandalism, or violence.

Almost any form of rebellion will do when one is simultaneously angry and starved for some measure of acceptance.

When the Heat Rises

Mark and Brenda Johnson are prime examples of parents with the beautiful house, the well-tended lawn, and the troubled home. As we explored the problems, we made the additional discovery that first-grader Amy's seeming tranquility was deceiving. She, too, had a rising level of anger only waiting to find its expression.

Yes, we discovered that six-year-old Amy was also angry at her parents.

Both the Johnsons and the Perkinses thought their children should sense their parents' love intuitively. They should have "just known" that they were loved. The problem is that children don't "just know." They are no more telepathic than anyone else, and they're also less skilled than adults in understanding the nuances and unspoken gestures of complex relationships. Perception often trumps reality, and both Ann and Todd perceived a lack of love. That is, they felt ignored. Their feelings were based on the amount of time and emotional energy their parents invested in them.

Let's not judge today's parents too harshly; we need to understand their world, too. The truth is that you and I live with far too much stress in our daily lives. We are like hallway closets crammed with too many coats, boxes, and bundles. There are so many activities, so many issues, so many responsibilities, and so many emotions that the door is straining to come off its hinges; the closet has no more empty space. As soon as a child brings something else to the closet—some problem, some momentary need, perhaps some simple request for affection—that closet of everyday life cannot accommodate another bundle. Our lives are filled to bursting, and we lack the resiliency and the emotional space to deal calmly with normal childhood behaviors.

It's not so easy to hold a family and a career together simultaneously today, not to mention the other many responsibilities and obligations parents may have: the demands of aging parents, personal medical concerns or physical limitations, church, the school PTA, a circle of friends all hovering around wanting something. Many parents don't have the energy or the perseverance to cover every single base.

In particular, let's consider the single-parent family. Many people believe that one person can't handle the multitude of needs that a home requires. But I have seen countless single parents give loving nurture and discipline to their children. Single parents can and do make it work, and I've seen the evidence of that. Two parents will always be the best option, of course. But the key to a successful family is not quantity of adults, but the focus that one or two parents chooses. A single parent can raise a child well and guide him or her through the "terrible teens" into responsible Christian adulthood, just as two parents can—if they adopt the right priorities in the home.

The issue, then, is priority. But when we have too much on our plates—indeed when we've become like the plate-juggler on the old variety show, spinning eight or ten items at once and trying to keep them all in the air—what is the first plate we're likely to drop? That is, which portion of life and responsibility will be the first to crash into pieces on the stage? It will usually be the one most immediate, the one right in front of our noses, the one we take for granted: the family.

After all, we don't want to provoke work supervisors, church leaders, or peers. But children and spouses will forgive us one more time. They will understand, won't they?

They will indeed—at least at first. When we push family concerns away in favor of some other urgent requirement, our children may understand up to a point in time. They may even forgive us seventy times seven. But eventually resentment begins to build. The pressure of the anger begins to rise. And when the frustration of children reaches the boiling point, we may be the first to feel the heat and the last to understand why.

Redeeming the Time

You've heard the buzzwords: "quality time." The phrase implies that there are different varieties of time, as if time comes in several flavors. It doesn't. Time is measured only in one direction, and on one instrument: the clock. It's marked off in seconds, in minutes, in days, and weekends. Time itself is what children crave; time with you, whatever the "flavor." Whether you're coaching a Little League team or simply working a jigsaw puzzle together, all that matters is that you have made yourself available. Time is the measurement by which we dole ourselves out to one other, not money spent or opportunities provided.

What the activity is means less than the time spent together. Spending time together is not really about the activity; it's about the experience of one another. You can learn a great deal about a child simply by building with blocks together, helping with homework, or working in the yard side by side. Your child learns a great deal about you as well, and empathy deepens into a more comprehensive love. Time spent says, "I love you," in a language that is profound and unfading. Being members of the greater Christian family, as outlined in 1 Corinthians 12, we understand that we cannot function fully and abundantly without each other. God has created us like parts of that jigsaw puzzle—pieces that must interlock to form a greater picture that will surprise and delight us. Thus we meet each other's needs emotionally, physically, psychologically, and spiritually within the context of family.

If we love each other, the mere necessities of living under the same roof will not begin to cover the depths of the relationship we will want to experience together. We'll be eager to enjoy each member of the family in a unique and fulfilling way. We will want to know our children deeply—their hopes, their dreams, their current fears. We will want to share intimately in the sacred pilgrimage of their lives. What activities should we choose? It really doesn't much matter, as long as we are laughing together, crying together, and growing together. Our children see the complexity of the lives we adults lead. They see all the activities and concerns.

We want to send them the clearest and most powerful message possible, and the message is this: You are worth far more than any of the rest. You are at the very center of my life, and you mean everything to me. Paraphrasing Paul's description of his love for God, we count everything else as rubbish compared to the overwhelming wealth of knowing those God has given us as family. Friendships, clubs, jobs, and nearly everything else will come and go in their seasons, but family is forever. We want to see it that way and live accordingly.

As we live out the beauty of family life as it was meant to be experienced, we find that it's not only our children who grow in wisdom and integrity. We, too, become people of stronger character. The family itself takes on a life of its own, profound and satisfying in spiritual dimension. As the years go by, we make life-long memories together in the most surprising of times—a moment at the dinner table or a hilarious episode during family vacation. Some of the events that seemed so important at the time, as well as the gifts and opportunities that cost the most money and energy, will fade away in the pleasant light of those small, perhaps playful moments that capture the real identity of family in some unexpected way. The expensive horseback riding lessons may pale in importance; but the impromptu picnic between father and daughter will never be forgotten by either.

You may verify this by reflecting over your own childhood memories. Which are the most precious ones? The pricey Christmas gifts or the priceless Christmas laughter? Do you best remember the words of permission granted for some endeavor, or the words of warmth and love in a moment of leisure?

The Johnsons and Perkinses discovered something that delighted and fulfilled them. They found that they could find time for family after all—quantity time, quality time, or whatever label we might choose to give it. Just making themselves available for counseling sessions proved that they had the time and the heart.

Counseling time can be painful, but family time together isn't painful at all. We discover there's no more satisfying commitment to make, and we wonder how any other activity could have crowded it out.

Learning to Communicate

It will come as no surprise to you that clear communication is essential to positive family life. Just as it's a key in marriage, it's a key in parenting.

As a matter of fact, it's also a key in business or any other endeavor that includes functioning in concert with other human beings. But in business, we might communicate with some formality; we might write memos and carefully worded letters. Family communication must be more honest and personal than that. We need to strive for a level of transparency and authenticity that may be a challenge for some of us. And we need to communicate positive and enriching words at every possible opportunity.

We're often together in the times when we're all tired and preoccupied with the earlier events of the day. We don't make the effort to smile and share a positive word. Aaron, who took part in a survey of 1,055 teenagers, expressed that sentiment. He observed, "Even when my parents are here, it's like they're not here, because they don't have any time." Although Aaron eats dinner with his parents, he said, "We never talk about anything. Maybe school. A lot of times, they're paranoid about my friends. They always get on my case when I come home."[1]

Family communication isn't the same as the kind that goes on in boardrooms or church planning meetings. Certain religious circles have advocated a "chain-of-command" approach, one that reminds us more of a battlefield than a family room. Military units have their reasons for depersonalizing communication, but it's doubtful that we need to do that with our spouses and children. Yet some Christian leaders set up rigid structures for father, mother, and children to follow to the letter. The father ends up like a general. He is the only one who truly carries any significant responsibilities. The wife and kids who are "down the line" need only follow his orders. It may be an effective way to defend a province, but not to build a family.

What inspired this chain-of-command approach? It seems to have been a rather direct outgrowth of the turbulent 1960s, when increased permissiveness and antiwar demonstrations caused alarm. During the same period of time, the world of psychology was dominated by the idea of behavior modification, a stimulus-response model based on experimentation with laboratory rats. The idea was that we can condition anyone to do anything, using positive or negative reinforcement. When that stream of thought was applied to family counseling, we saw the popularity of a "spare the rod and spoil the child" emphasis in parenting. In my judgment, this amounted to treating children as laboratory rats, applying punishment to modify behavior. A subtle but powerful change in parenting and parent-child relationships began to set in.

This punishment-based movement represented a profound misunderstanding of normal adolescent behavior and emotions. The idea was that all the nation's problems could be chalked up to parental permissiveness, and that we simply needed to tighten up the discipline in the home as a cure-all. Empathy, clear communication, and working together for family decisions were "too soft." Instead, a family hierarchy of strict authority was advocated.

The key issue in this change is subtle but absolutely crucial. Who is responsible for a child's behavior: the parents, the children, or both of them working together? In the chain-of-command, it was all up to the parents—ultimately the father in particular. He simply had to "condition" the child through spanking, punishment, and other forms of discipline. Instead of the child learning to decide wisely, the emphasis was on the parent "erasing" wrong behavior by means of negative reinforcement.

The mutual model of responsibility, on the other hand, sends the message that parents and children must work together. The parent is saying to the child, "You have the power to make decisions. We must work together, and I will guide you and help you in learning to make the wise decision."

Has an increase in strict discipline solved our problems? I would say the answer is a strong negative one. We now observe a generation of children who refuse to take responsibility for their behavior. Treating children like laboratory animals is depersonalizing. It results in distrust, resentment, and a lack of close-knit affection. The emphasis is on firmness rather than communication, on "because I said so" rather than "come, let us reason together."

Then, when the spirit of rebellion inevitably breaks out, we have a vicious cycle. That is, parents don't stop to question the discipline itself; they merely apply more of it when things go wrong. The stricter the parents' treatment, the greater their wrath, and the greater the lack of love and support, the angrier the children grow. They experience problems with that anger more and more as they move into the world, all of which causes them to rebel even more against authority. And the end result is a young adult permanently at war: at war with parents, at war with morality, at war with other people, at war with church, at war with laws and government, and at war with every other social structure. We produce a generation of children who become islands unto themselves, frustrated and isolated because they can't live in harmony with a world of other lonely soldiers.

It's also possible to err disastrously in the other extreme. Some dismayed educators believe we can solve our problems by simply making the children "feel good." Thus we have the self-esteem movement. A child receives special commendation for behaving in a pleasant manner—something that should be expected rather than rewarded. But is mere self-esteem effective in creating the right behavior? The trial of the Menendez brothers occurred to much publicity in 1993. These siblings had murdered their parents. Writing in *National Review*, Stuart Goldman suggests that the Menendez murders and the trial are an example of the self-esteem philosophy gone awry:

In the cosmology of the self-help movement, all human failure stems from our lack of ability to love ourselves; the worst thing a person can have is a bad case of low self-esteem. ... In a world where morality is dictated by therapists rather than God, where evil is discounted as a myth, where feeling good is the end-all and be-all, they can be comforted by the thought that murdering an "abusive" parent is not only permissible—it is healthy.[2]

We need not impose military rigidity upon our households, and we can do much better than blandly celebrating every example of proper behavior. What we can substitute for both extremes is personal and loving interaction with our children, coming alongside them to guide and train them in lives of wisdom and integrity. We can teach them respect for other people and for themselves. At all times we can show them how to take personal responsibility for their behavior.

Before we turn to the specifics of dealing with anger in our children, there is one other general course of action to consider. It involves a tradition much ignored today: the greater circle of your extended family.

The Family Beyond Your Family

Parents cry out, "There isn't enough time! I have so many responsibilities, so many burdens. How can I give my children the time they need?"

I would like to suggest that relief may be available in a way that is particularly healthy and satisfying. Grandparents and other extended family members often enjoy taking an active role in the lives of their young relatives.

But what if grandparents, aunts, and uncles live far away? I see many cases of young families moving a great distance away from the home base, often for some business opportunity. They find themselves far removed from their base of support, where friends and family are close at hand and ready to help. Moving away from an entire support network is a great sacrifice to make, and perhaps an unnecessary one in many cases. Children could use the extra love and attention they would have received. We could use it, too.

I realize this is a thorny issue without any easy solutions. After all, the old friends who are our age are raising their own families, and they have their own stress issues. And perhaps parents don't express the desire to have more time with their grandchildren. Their message may come across as, "I raised my family. Now go raise yours and let me rest."

However, there may be some answers. If family members do want to be closer, someone may decide to make a geographical move to foster more involvement in extended family. If you can't move, perhaps the grandparents can.

If all else fails, there is one solution that is always available. You can build a strong new network of loving and nurturing friends. Perhaps you'll find them in your neighborhood. Perhaps you'll find them in your church or within the school community. In past generations, children were enriched by a wealth of relationships through aunts, uncles, cousins, and grandparents. As they grow up, most children come to cherish these extended family relationships more and more. But if you lack that outer circle, you must build one through friends who have much in common with you; friends who can keep your children safe in the event of an emergency; friends who can offer a shoulder to cry on or a word of advice; friends who can, in turn, count on your friendship in their own times of need.

This is a lifestyle issue. You may have to take the costly time and effort to find a friendlier church or to meet more of the other parents in your neighborhood. You may have to put away your pride, humble yourself, and sit down with your parents or in-laws and admit you could really use their assistance. You may need to come to the simple realization that you weren't designed by God to carry every burden alone. That's why he made friends and family. None of this is easy, but after you decide what you most want for your family and who can best contribute the gifts of time and love to your children, the sacrifices are sure to be well worth the cost.

What is the alternative? You can continue stretching yourself beyond the resources of your time, physical and emotional energy, and abilities to be everything your family needs. This vain endeavor will take its toll on both you and your family. It will strain a marriage; it will frustrate children; it will bring you to increased impatience and anger of your own.

Because children have no defense against parental anger, their hurt and frustration sinks deep inside and festers. To have one or more adults nearby who can love and care for your child will give you relief and will also soothe your child's feelings, especially if you succumb to the pressures and express anger that you'll later regret.

We would do well to take Dorothy Law Nolte's familiar poem to heart:

Children Learn What They Live

If a child lives with criticism,
he learns to condemn.
If a child lives with hostility,
he learns to fight.
If a child lives with ridicule,
he learns to be shy.
If a child lives with shame,
he learns to feel guilty.
If a child lives with tolerance,
he learns to be patient.
If a child lives with encouragement,
he learns confidence.
If a child lives with praise,
he learns to appreciate.
If a child lives with fairness,
he learns justice.
If a child lives with security,
he learns to have faith.
If a child lives with approval,
he learns to like himself.
If a child lives with acceptance and friendship,
he learns to find love in the world.

4

Love without Limits

Question: As an adult, how do you learn something new? What is the most typical way your mind uploads new information and installs it in that hard drive behind your eyes and between your ears?

People learn in various ways. Perhaps you ask a question and listen carefully to the response. Perhaps you attend a seminar and take careful notes. In most cases, your medium for learning is words. Perhaps you learn about the Bible in church by sitting in a pew, hands folded, listening to the pastor speak for 30 minutes or more. Words are our mental software.

But what about a five-year-old boy? Does he learn in the same way?

Any parent who has grappled with a squirming child during the worship service could answer that question immediately!

How are young children taught in your church or school? They learn with words, but to a much greater extent, they learn through activity. They sit in circles where everyone can be engaged and involved. They pass around objects to see and touch. All people learn through doing, but it's particularly true of children. They are behavioral in their learning orientation, while adults are verbal.

Let's apply this insight to the subject of family love. How do parents express their affection toward their children, and how do children learn they are loved? When kids are very small and cannot yet talk, parents instinctively understand that they need to hug and to touch, to smile and to laugh; they are careful to act out their love physically. But somehow, as children grow, parents carelessly fall back to mere verbal communication and the occasional statement, "I love you," to express feelings.

We do need to say those three powerful words, and we need to say them frequently. But words are not enough. All of our lives together as family make up one ongoing dialogue, or more precisely the complex answer to the Big Question: "Do you love me?" Children ask it every day, in every way. They may not express it in words, but they are constantly in need of the answer to that question.

But why is that so? A husband says to his wife, "What do you mean, 'do you love me?' Of course I love you! I said those words in front of the church and before God. I've told you in the past, several times. How many times must I keep saying it?"

The answer is regularly. We must express love with consistency, one of the most important words you'll find in this chapter. And children need that consistent expression the most. And while you can tell your spouse of your love in words, you must show it to your children. They need demonstrations of your love to maintain a strong sense of your affection.

It's important to keep in mind that ongoing question of family life. Even when your children are acting out their anger, pouting, behaving in some unacceptable fashion, they are asking, "Do you love me?" The subtext is, "Do you love me enough to be patient with me?"

We certainly don't like the form of the question. You might now be asking, "Why can't my children just come to me and ask me about this? Why should I endure the stormy behavior?" But a child, of course, lacks your emotional perspective. A child expresses every emotion immaturely, including through anger. A child "vents" and releases aggression.

No parent enjoys putting up with these demonstrations, but the truth is that such episodes are the raw material we must use for the purpose of molding them into mature adults. These episodes are a starting point for guiding children into more mature expressions of their emotions. As a matter of fact, demonstrations of anger are supremely teachable moments. Sadly enough, we seldom seize the moment to teach the lesson.

If we're going to help our children move along in normal emotional development, we must accept their angry emotions—not as desirable, but as normal. They are the starting point, and we must start somewhere. We certainly can't afford to react in our own inappropriate expressions of anger. We teach entirely the wrong lesson then, and our children will carry it with them through their lives.

When children are new in the world, we expect behavior appropriate to the age. We expect diapers to be wet and baby food to be hurled across the room from the high chair. We also expect to be dealing with our own anger occasionally. But the anger of others is difficult for most of us to handle, even in the children we love. Most parents struggle to deal with anger in the right way. In their frustration, they often fail to supply unconditional love and acceptance at that very moment when it is most needed. The angry child needs love to deal with whatever the crisis may be—frustration with a toy or with a sibling—but our anger often sends the message, "I do not love you when you're angry." We do love them, of course, but children draw their conclusions from our behavior.

I am a parent, too, and I had to confront these same frustrating challenges with our children. I found it useful to frequently remind myself of several rather obvious facts:

• They are children, and they will act accordingly.
• Childish behavior is often unpleasant.
• To love my children, unpleasant behavior and all, is to encourage their growth.
• To love them only when they're loveable is to convince them my love has strings attached. This stifles their development; it breeds insecurity.
• I share with my children the responsibility for their behavior and development.
• If I love my children unconditionally, I build security, self-content, and self-control.

- If I love them based on their performance, I build the feeling of incompetence. Their best will never seem enough. I will be breeding insecurity, anxiety, and low self-esteem.
- For all these reasons, I share equally with my children the responsibility for their total growth.[1]

Craving Unconditional Love

Love is not instinctive; it works more on the mirror principle. A mirror is the plain reflection of what the light casts upon it. Children merely reflect the love they receive. In other words, children must learn to love in the same way they must learn to feed themselves, walk, or ride a bicycle. But if parents don't demonstrate love, children will never know what love is and never offer it themselves. Love must be learned.

On the other hand, as you pour out your love upon your children, they will reflect it back upon you in a beautiful way. You will see your love in them, just as they have seen in you the life and the love they can give. And don't forget that mirrors are often imperfect. They can be cracked or coated in dust. Paul spoke of seeing God in a mirror dimly, due to our own weaknesses clouding the glass: "Now we see but a poor reflection as in a mirror; then we shall see face to face. Now I know in part; then I shall know fully, even as I am fully known" (1 Cor. 13:12).

The more confusion and rebellion there is in our lives, the less we are able to know our God, and the dustier the glass that lies between us. But one day, in a perfect world beyond this one, the glass will sparkle until it becomes invisible. The dazzling light of God's love will shine through, and we will know and partake of it perfectly.

In the same way, our weaknesses and failings can damage the glass into which our children gaze. If our view of God is obscured, how much more imperfect is our children's view of us? Quite often, we love them abundantly, perfectly—but we have our bad moments, too. We must never take parental love for granted, but constantly clean and polish the glass so the love can shine through. When some issue hurts our relationship with our kids, we must discover how to wipe that residue away to keep the channels of trust and communication clear. That's our way of "dusting the mirror" of love.

But perhaps we're brooding over some issue from work or outside relationships; we're not fully attentive to our children in those moments, and they know it. On those occasions, children aren't certain what they are seeing in the mirror. They might get mixed signals. The image seems to shift from warm and attentive to cool and distant. If this is the case too often, children learn not to trust, and love is not possible where there is no trust. Children will fail to move toward completeness and a positive self-concept.

As David Seamands explains in his book *Healing for Damaged Emotions*, children always "know in part" (again reflecting Paul's words). They never have the full understanding of any issue, and they're often less knowing than we assume. Maturity is all about growing toward a deeper, fuller, face-to-face understanding. Think about your own growth process, and you'll recall that you came to understand, over the years, the unique ways your parents, and even your siblings, expressed their love. Perhaps your father was less verbal in his expression, and you weren't always certain about his affection. In time, you learned to "read" his reactions, and you knew when he was proud of you. Perhaps your mother expressed her love more through human touch.

We have looked into those mirrors and made assumptions about ourselves based upon what we have seen. Our children are now doing the same thing, moment by moment. Seamands writes, "These reflections tell us not only who we are, but also what we are going to become. As the reflections gradually become part of us, we take on the shape of the person we see in the family looking glass."[2]

A Rock-Solid Foundation

Childhood is a time of building, brick by brick, from a strong foundation. We are the builders, and God is the architect. Step by step, year by year, God builds the comfortable and elegant rooms that he himself will move into when the child becomes an adult.

We must realize that the time of building comes only once. Mislaid bricks and careless construction can cause long-lasting damage. On the other hand, we can build a powerful, rock-solid self-identity in children. We can guide them to becoming godly temples that will withstand any storm that adulthood blows their way. Each morning, we should take in hand the daily bricks or problems, issues, and opportunities, and place them lovingly and sensitively, as if we were Solomon constructing God's temple. After all, our children are eternal souls.

What will happen if your children look into the mirror and conclude that their personal worth as human beings is low? Their words and actions will never really matter; they are not loved, and there is no reason for them to create loving lives. Once this self-understanding takes root within them, it will become very difficult—in some cases impossible, short of a miracle—for them to feel the love and acceptance of God and to find their rightful places in God's service.[3]

When children cannot become what they know deep inside they should be, when they cannot be themselves—when life is little more than the House of Mirrors at the carnival, where all the images are mocking, distorted, and unforgiving—they become angry.

What about your own struggle to love and to be loved? If you have reached a place in life where you are free to be yourself and to express yourself, you know that victory was hard-won. You have directed your own anger at those who should have loved you, who should have accepted you with no strings attached, who should have reached out a hand to make your journey a bit easier. Hopefully, you've worked through those emotions. Surely you would not purposefully create the same traumatic challenges for your own child. And yet many parents never make that connection between their own struggle for love and that of their children. Having craved unconditional love for themselves, they end up withholding it from the little ones who depend upon them.

Limited, conditional love will make life difficult for you as well as for your children. Love with strings attached will never work, so that you'll constantly find yourself baffled by your children's behavior. You won't know how to guide them. Conditional love means asking of your children what they are incapable of providing—for who can truly earn love through perfect behavior? Family life can never be rewarding in such a setting.

But unconditional love is as enriching for you as it is for your children. You are free to love without setting parameters—to love as God loves, "just because." Your parenting will be strong and confident, and you will always have the grace and wisdom to meet your children's needs.

Parents Who Provoke

Nearly everyone knows one particular commandment. God gave Moses the commandment to honor one's father and mother, and most of us grew up with its words ringing in our ears whenever we rolled our eyes or balked at a command. Two thousand years later, Paul reminded the Ephesians of that commandment:

Children, obey your parents in the Lord, for this is right. "Honor your father and mother"—which is the first commandment with a promise—"that it may go well with you and that you may enjoy long life on the earth" (Eph. 6:1–3).

The Ephesians may not have needed that reminder any more than you. But Paul added a disclaimer in verse four that everyone needs. I wonder how often your parents quoted this one? Let's hear it in several translations and paraphrases:

Fathers, again, must not goad your children to resentment, but give them the instruction, and the correction, which belong to a Christian upbringing (NEB).

Fathers, provoke not your children to wrath: but bring them up in the nurture and admonition of the Lord (KJV).

You parents, too, must stop exasperating your children, but continue to bring them up with the sort of education and counsel the Lord approves (WMS).

And you fathers, don't make your children angry, but raise them by letting the Lord train and correct them (BECK).

And now a word to you fathers. Don't make your children angry by the way you treat them. Rather, bring them up with the discipline and instruction approved by the Lord (NLB).

Fathers, don't exasperate your children by coming down hard on them. Take them by the hand and lead them in the way of the Master (TM).

I can imagine Paul making his pastoral rounds in the city of Ephesus, sitting in the living rooms of the young Christians' homes and hearing the shouted parent-child arguments in the hall. Some things never change. Mothers and fathers will always struggle to be patient with their children. So when Paul was writing his letter, he added the other side of the story. He quoted the commandment of the Old Testament and anointed it with the grace of the New. Children must obey, but parents must manage their ability to do so through avoiding provocation. It's a two-way street.

If Paul visited your home, would he say, "Ease up on your kids"? A lot of provoking goes on in homes that profess to be Christian. Have you witnessed the following scenes?

- A three-year-old girl picks a flower and presents it to her mother. But the flower has come from the neighbor's yard, so the mother slaps the child, discards the loving gift, and offers a stern lecture.

- In the ice cream parlor, a father bellows at his young son when he sees a bit of vanilla drifting from the boy's cone onto his shirt.

- A mother asks her daughter, "Why can't you play the piano better, like your sister does?"

- A father hollers from a window to his son, "Get your friends out of our yard. They are ruining the grass!"

- A child starts to wander away from his mother in a crowded mall. The mother jerks him back roughly, yelling, "You stay right here where I put you!"

• A father buys a new bicycle for his son. But the next day, he's screaming at the boy to keep it out of the driveway. The mixed messages are hurtful and confusing.

Imagine Paul arriving for a visit as a weekend guest in your home. Would he encourage you to let your children run roughshod over all the rules? Of course not. He would take them aside and remind them gently of Moses' commandment to honor our parents. But I have a feeling he would also speak to you privately and encourage you to season your discipline with gentle grace. He would remind you that the best guidance is packaged in love rather than anger.

Training in Focus

If you have read my first book, *How to Really Love Your Child*, you already know of my emphasis on focus in loving and training your children. This takes the form of eye contact, physical contact, and focused attention in both listening and responding to your children. Focused love is a way of impressing deeply how much you love them.

Why not apply the concept of laser focus to this very chapter? We'll hone in on each of the important areas I've just mentioned, especially as they apply to dealing with our children's anger. We can all focus our love on a smiling, affectionate, and obedient child. But when the storms come and the rebellion rises in our homes, we need laser-strong patience and concentration to avoid giving in to our own anger. That's why the following areas are so important. Let's shed a little laser light on the key points of parent-child contact.

Eye Contact

Have you ever noticed the subtle but powerful place of eye contact in human relationships? We teach our children to look adults right in the eye when conversing with them. But do we follow our own advice? What are our eyes saying when we lend them our ears?

It's important to look pleasantly into the eyes of your child while he or she is speaking to you. It sounds simple, and it is. But it's also a profoundly meaningful and complex behavior that becomes a medium for unspoken messages sent back and forth. When you speak to a friend at a party and see your companion scanning the crowd over your shoulder, what message do you receive? What do you gather about your friend's regard for you?

You can see the gravity of this simple, nearly indiscernible behavior of the pupil and iris. I can tell you that most parents feel secure about their "eye messages" with their children; I can also tell you that most parents aren't doing nearly as good a job as they believe, according to our research. How about you?

Eye contact is delightful when the child is a cooing baby and we're trying to make her laugh. But eye contact is treacherous when the child is 13 years old, enraged, and verbally attacking you in a loud voice at the end of your long and tiring day. What will your eyes say then? Yet there's the hard part: this is the very time when your response is the most critical. This is the daily watershed of the parent-child relationship, when you will either successfully teach a lesson in handling anger or make the situation much worse than it is, particularly in the long run. The stakes are high indeed.

I imagine you may be feeling some anxiety as you think about this problem. Yes, you need all the help you can get during that moment of crisis, when the hot water reaches the boiling point. What can you do?

For one thing, you can bolster your defenses by employing self-talk during such an outburst. This is a technique for maintaining self-control when we're angry. Here is a series of reminders you can mentally check off:

√ It is normal for your child to express anger verbally to you, even if ...

√ It is unpleasant to deal with the anger, because ...

√ The anger is the only opportunity you'll have for teaching how to control it.

Self-talk has considerable power. You have the ability to remain focused on giving your son or daughter pleasant eye contact during this moment of crisis. Regardless of your child's actions, regardless of words, you need to maintain eye contact. If your child glares at you, it will be tempting to glance away. We say, "If looks could kill …" but after all, they can't. This is only a moment of desperation. If you break eye contact, you're only increasing the anger by sending the wrong signal about your relationship.

Nearly any parent of a teenager has passed through the "grunt stage." That's the period of emotional withdrawal when your child offers little beyond an irritating grunt. At such times, when healthy communication is on the wane, your child will be the one avoiding eye contact. This reversal makes you the one who is frustrated. You will be even further tempted to withhold loving eye contact.

Don't withhold it. Maintain your self-talk; keep a firm grip on your perspective. Remind yourself that this, too, shall pass; it's a storm countless parents have already weathered, and the important thing is that you love your child just as much when he or she is difficult. You will look your child right in the eye, even when it's toughest to do so, and love your son or daughter through your eye contact with laser intensity.

If you can do that, you're passing one of the toughest tests that parenting has to offer. You will see and feel the difference. In managing your own anger and frustration, you will be teaching your child how to do the same.

Physical Contact

During all the grunts and locked bedroom doors, when your child is the one to withhold eye contact, another tool is still at your disposal. It's the tool of physical contact.

We all know that human touch is absolutely essential in raising children. We all know the yearning to touch and to be touched, first in regard to our parents, then in regard to a spouse.

Yet research consistently tells us that few children receive sufficient physical contact to keep their emotional tanks full. During the happy times, it's easy to embrace, to slap the back, to grasp the hand, to find every opportunity to touch one another. But during the emotional storms, both parent and child may retreat to their corners. They may shrink away awkwardly. And once again, as you might have guessed, this is the very time when it is most costly to do so. This is the time when physical contact is essential. It may even save the day.

Your teenager may be avoiding you. He or she may mumble or grunt and may look in the opposite direction when you're making every effort to communicate. But even here, in the grunt stage, you can use physical contact to express in a deep and powerful way that you love your children no less than ever. Your child may not be angry at you, but simply engrossed in reflections about the confusing social world he or she is newly experiencing. Your teen isn't fully aware of your presence and your concern. But when you reach out a gentle hand, offer a quick touch to the shoulder, or lightly pat the arm, for instance, you're sending a message that might, in words, be disregarded. Even in an apparent self-involved trance, your child will respond to loving physical contact.

Be sensitive, of course. An aggressive full embrace, sudden and undesired, might only serve to make matters worse. You know your children well enough to realize, at a given moment, what would be well received. If your child is particularly angry, eye contact alone might be all you have to offer—other than the visible testimony of loving patience.

Focused Attention

What other tools in a parent's arsenal can be focused to laser intensity? Our attention, of course.

Attention is simply another word for time. There's no more precious resource given to us than the minutes and hours in a day. When we choose to invest them in companionship with our children, they cannot help but feel the love we demonstrate. This is your way of making a child know for a certainty that, at least for a little while, he or she is the most important person in the world to you. It is also a one-on-one experience—just one parent and one child together. During those moments, many wonderful things can happen. We can maintain eye-to-eye contact. We can use physical touch to our advantage. We find that we hear better, express ourselves better, and come to know each other more deeply. Nothing in the world can take the place of focused attention, but it comes at a high price. It is purchased by the coin of our personal time, which naturally has its limits.

You may not feel particularly motivated to provide focused attention. Maybe your teenager has been moody and unappealing in conversation and demeanor. If you're honest with yourself, your child may be the last person in the world you want to spend your time with. As you've guessed, your feelings are pretty good indicators that focused attention is exactly what both of you need.

You may want to take your child somewhere away from the home (a neutral field) where you can speak and hear one another more clearly. You will also want to ask yourself whether your child's emotional tank is full. Has he or she been receiving the love a child craves? If your child has been sullen or unresponsive, focused attention may help you get to the bottom of the mystery so you can make reparations.

Don't expect instant miracles; bring a good supply of patience along. Silence does not always imply hostility. Many of your child's moods, changing like the weather, may have nothing whatsoever to do with you. Teenagers are preoccupied with many new problems, and they also need time and space to pull themselves together after periods of anger. Parents may be in a hurry to get everything back to normal at home and may pressure kids to "let us see that smile that used to light up the room." But leave off that pressure; respect a bit of distance. Eventually, your child will open up and may even allow meaningful conversation and a resolution to the big issue that inspired the anger. In any case, he or she will appreciate your treating privacy with respect, adult-style.

Let's look at a good example of the principles we're discussing.

Our son David, 13 at the time, was invited by his friend Joe to spend the night. Joe's parents had recently divorced; he and his mother lived nearby, and we considered them good neighbors. But on this particular occasion, we found out that Joe's mother was having a boyfriend over for the night. As much as we liked Joe and his mother, we couldn't allow David to stay there overnight.

David couldn't understand our decision. He was furious and wouldn't cool down. As he saw it, we were condemning his friend's mother and household. Our son slept at home that night and carried his anger over into the morning. I refused to react to his behavior, asking him instead if he'd like to have breakfast at his favorite restaurant. As I'd expected, that was an offer he couldn't refuse.

As we waited for our food, David opened up a bit and told me how hurt he was by our decision to keep him at home. Then he asked me what I thought about the behavior of Joe's mother.

Now I had the right opportunity, because I had saved my opinion until he'd asked for it. I told him that his mother and I loved our neighbors as much as he did. We were still sad about the divorce and about Joe's father moving away. I also explained that the lifestyle of Joe's mother was her own business—though as David's father, I would not be doing my job if I exposed him to such a situation. David listened attentively and eventually came to understand our position.

We might have had it all out in the heat of anger. Instead, focused attention helped us resolve the impasse in a cool and sensible fashion. A family dispute was transformed to a teaching experience.

Emotions in the Tank

We've talked about your child's emotional tank, and you must keep it full like the tank on an automobile. In the context of unconditional love, the tools of eye contact, physical contact, and focused attention are simply ways of effectively filling your child's emotional tank. Your child needs unconditional love, demonstrated in many ways, to become what he or she wants to be, can be, and should be.

As we said at the beginning of this chapter, consistency is the key. If children have to wonder from day to day if they can trust their parents' love and if there is any point in trying to please parents, they will be discouraged from doing their best. They will have doubts about their own worth.

David Seamands writes of a young man named Bob who grew up in a home where the rallying cry was "Measure up." He learned early in life that measuring up was the basis for his being loved and accepted by his parents. And that's what he set out to do. Bob's parents did as so many of us do at times:

> So subtly we withhold our full affection and love until we see that our children are striving at their highest level. Instead of affirming them at the level where they are, we think we are helping them to "do a little bit better." So whatever they do— eating their food or using good manners or making grades or living the Christian life on their own age level—we give our children the promise of our approval and love if only they will do a little bit better. Love becomes something just around the corner, just a hope away. The present level of achievement is subtly downgraded and belittled. We think we are saying, "We love you and want you to do better." Too often it comes across to our children as, "We will love you when you measure up," or "We will love you and be pleased with you, if only you'll do a little bit better."[4]

Your self-esteem in life will be a simple product of the extent to which you are loved unconditionally.[5] You know this from your own experience, and the same is true for your child.

> Unconditional love has two fundamental qualities: (1) It is given without regard for the objective value of the person or thing which is loved; (2) It is given without any strings or conditions attached ... That's the kind of love which can turn your life around and raise your self-esteem level to new heights. When you find love like that, you are set free to become the person you were meant to be in all your uniqueness. And when you experience yourself in the middle of that kind of freedom, you can't help feeling good about who you find yourself to be ... We want to be loved *for no good reason at all.*[6]

In *Make Anger Your Ally*, Dr. Warren suggests how you can know you've found this kind of love. When you realize beyond certainty that nothing you could ever do—nothing in the world—would separate you from the other person's love, you have arrived. You've found a love without limits, and it frees you from what Dr. Carl Rogers calls "conditions of worth." Rogers explains that we no longer have to perform to earn another person's love. There are no longer any price tags other than to be who we are. Then we can set out on that fulfilling journey toward knowing ourselves deeply, with no pressure to fulfill the expectations of others and be something we are not.[7]

The freedom of unconditional love breeds a powerful sense of self in our children, and it frees them to be the children, then the adults, they can potentially become. Someone with a strong sense of self has the security to handle his or her own anger and to transform the moment to something positive and edifying.

Your home can be a place where such "growth moments" happen on a regular basis. Your children can learn not only from the words you say, but the words you leave unsaid; not only from how you act, but how you refrain from acting. They can learn from your patience with their imperfections. They can learn from your sacrifice of offering time and attention, from your pain in striving to make eye contact when it's difficult to do so. They can see the strength with which you calm the waters of a storm, and in time they'll be certain to find that same strength within themselves.

In your home, your children can learn how much they mean to you, to God, and to themselves. They can experience, in a love without limits, an unconditional acceptance we hope and pray they will ultimately experience to its fullest in the One who made them:

> Who shall separate us from the love of Christ? Shall trouble or hardship or persecution or famine or nakedness or danger or sword?
>
> No, in all these things we are more than conquerors through him who loved us. For I am convinced that neither death nor life, neither angels nor demons, neither the present nor the future, nor any powers, neither height nor depth, nor anything else in all creation, will be able to separate us from the love of God that is in Christ Jesus our Lord (Rom. 8:35, 37–39).

5

Anger Unmasked

You couldn't find a more appealing five-year-old than Jimmy. Every member of the kindergarten staff enjoys interacting with him. Jimmy is outgoing yet composed, curious yet restrained, fully engaged in the class activities and socially well adjusted. If all the kids were like Jimmy, teaching kindergarten would be a breeze.

At least it seems that way until the playground incident.

Everyone knows five-year-olds can be wild when released into the outdoors on a spring day. So nobody particularly panics when Tony, another boy, collides with Jimmy near the swing-set and knocks him on the ground. But Jimmy leaps to his feet, tackles the startled Tony, and pounds him with blow after blow before the playground supervisor can pull him away.

At the end of the day, Tony has one cut over his eye and two angry parents. Jimmy, it turns out, was ill earlier in the day. He has been unable to keep a meal in his stomach. Jimmy is contrite over his temperamental outburst, and he apologizes to his friend Tony. But what is the source of such spontaneous rage?

Under normal circumstances, Jimmy has no problems controlling his anger. He knows what he has done on the playground today is wrong. But on a day when his system is fighting a virus, he has less strength available for controlling his emotions.

Several miles away, we find another well-liked, well-behaved kindergartener. Mario is bright, happy, and popular with the other children. He is particularly good about sharing his toys. But suddenly, the little boy enters a phase of repeatedly soiling his pants. Mario is just as puzzled by this development as his parents and teachers, and he suffers a great deal of embarrassment over what the adults angrily call "baby stuff." But no matter what anyone says, he can't seem to control his soiling.

In Mario, we see a case of anger that is not a feeling. After all, the kindergartener doesn't feel angry. He has no idea what causes the physical response of wetting his pants. He doesn't show any obvious behavioral signs of anger, but anger is the controlling factor just the same. Issues at home and in the classroom have disturbed Mario more than he or any adult has realized. The teachers have bragged on him for not showing anger when other children seize his toys, but they should think again. Anger can be invisible and even unfelt. Eventually, it will find an outlet.

Six-year-old Luisa is a verbal child who fluently expresses her feelings, especially in conversation. Luisa is quite the talker, and her mother is proud of her child's advanced verbal ability. But the first-grader is advanced in other ways, too—less appealing ones. She is, in fact, adept at using her speaking skills to manipulate her mother.

When Luisa is getting what she wants, she is "sugar and spice, and everything nice." But if she runs into the word "no," she becomes hostile very quickly. She complains, whines, argues, and raises her voice until Mom finally becomes angry, too. Mom begins yelling back at her daughter, and this only raises the temperature of an already boiling pot. When the scene becomes unpleasant enough, Luisa's mother does one of two things: she either gives the child what she wants, or she overreacts even more intensely to Luisa's anger and imposes a severe punishment.

That's how the cycle goes: confrontations increase in frequency as frustration builds up on either side. Luisa's mother isn't quite sure what she should do. It seems to her that the child should be allowed to vent her emotions because she's always heard that it would be unhealthy for a child to "bottle up" her anger. This, of course, is the popular notion that a child should be allowed to release all emotions with total freedom. Mom fears that if Luisa is forced to bury her feelings inside, her personal development will be damaged. (The "ventilation myth" is debunked in a fine book called *The Cycle of Violence* by Suzanne R. Steinmetz.) Anger should not be suppressed or repressed, but it should be handled in an appropriate way.

It Comes with the Age

Jimmy, then, is overcome by aggression. Mario is a victim of unconsciously motivated behavior. And Luisa vents until the household is in chaos. These are three common approaches we observe in a child's handling of anger.

Jimmy, Mario, and Luisa are emotionally immature simply because they are children. Anger arrives in life far before we possess the skills to handle it, and some of us, unfortunately, never do. Children lack the capabilities to deal properly with their emotions in the beginning. That observation goes without saying, but the truth is that we tend to forget. It's unpleasant to deal with poorly controlled anger, and our frustration obscures our simple realization that children are immature and are going to struggle to control their anger.

Anger cannot be avoided; it must be met and channeled appropriately. If we're going to teach our children about emotional maturity, we must start somewhere. And that particular "somewhere" is not an enjoyable place to be. Children experience anger and the anger finds expression, commonly through venting and aggression. Unconscious expressions of anger involve suppression, and these expressions, of course, are the ones parents should particularly watch out for.

We must, then, accept the inevitable. This doesn't mean we have to enjoy unpleasant childish displays of anger, but we can at least take the first step of expecting these outbursts and acknowledging that they are ordinary. From there, our task is to train children to understand and control their anger, not immediately but gradually. They will not instantly learn to read or to swim or to play baseball, either. A reasonable goal, as I have come to believe, is for children to arrive at a place of maturity in expressing anger by the time they are 17. This means that parents will continually work at this task, dealing with children on the age level where they are.

Here are the two problems most parents encounter with that training process.

First, they lack the understanding of what skills and techniques to teach, since, as adults, they have their own issues in the field of anger management.

Second, they react poorly and in a damaging way when children behave like children. As we have seen, they have not accepted the fact that children will not handle anger with maturity. Parents, after all, have been known to vent their own emotions and express their own aggression—often in full view of their children. But they bring a double standard to their approach to anger in the home: "Do as we say, not as we do; we are the parents, and we will behave how we please." Mom and Dad should understand the ineffectiveness of teaching under those conditions, but they often fail to see the obvious.

Where do we begin? First, in this chapter, we will discover what anger is—we will "unmask" it, if we can. Then we will investigate the values of anger. And finally, we will close chapter 5 by inspecting some common patterns of family behavior. You may recognize your own home more than once.

In chapters 6 and 7, we will think about the subconscious and conscious expressions of anger that cause such havoc in increasing numbers of homes.

Anger, as we will see, is no simple topic. It's quite complex and thoroughly misunderstood by most people, even some lifelong students of the subject. What we can hope to accomplish in this book is a broad overview that will provide motivation for your further thinking, reading, and growth.

Those who read my book *How to Really Love Your Teenager* may remember the Anger Ladder, a visual aid for helping us consider the process of anger. I've included it at the end of the current chapter because it illustrates most of the common ways of expressing anger. It's not particularly important exactly how many rungs are on that ladder; what matters is the direction of the climb. We see a step-by-step progression from less acceptable forms of expressing anger to healthier behaviors, which are printed in capital letters.

I hope you will find the Anger Ladder to be a helpful reference point as you work through this book and work in the context of your own family situation.

Why So Angry?

What is it that sets you off emotionally? Have you ever paused to consider carefully what it is that stokes your fire?

The short answer is that you become angry because of the anxiety that results from some kind of threat to you or to someone important to you. That threat could be life threatening or merely annoying. It could be right in front of us or hidden and unacknowledged, clear or foggy. The thing challenging us could take the form of physical danger, ridicule, or perhaps the irritation that results from someone failing to fulfill some task you expected of that person.

A threat to you or your loved one triggers anxiety. Whether or not you realize it, anxiety is a gift from God in disguise, because the combination of fear and anger at an impending threat causes you to prepare certain personal faculties. Anxiety is a useful defense mechanism. Depending on the size of the threat, you may initially feel more fear or more anger.

Let's imagine you find yourself driving on an icy patch of road. You're anxious, fearful, but not angry. Imagine now that you have children, and your neighbor drives up and down the street at 60 miles per hour. Whenever you hear his engine, you feel that anxiety rise, along with both fear and a measure of anger. Every threat has different combinations of fear, anxiety, and anger.

The threat could be to your physical well being, your social standing, your family, your self-esteem, your economic security, your possessions, your inner peace of mind, your desires, your beliefs, or your relationships. It's simply a matter of whether you or anything (or anyone) you value is at risk. And of course, life dictates that there is constantly some risk in play. We move through our days carrying significant anxieties over crime, the economy, terrorism, and any number of other concerns. It's not surprising that our instincts for self-preservation run high.

Why should we discuss this subject? It's important to specifically identify the sources of anger and anxiety, since not all are created equal. Some anxieties are useful anxieties and some harmful. We also need to understand exactly what is going on within us in relation to our fears and worries. In his book, *Coping with Your Anger: A Christian Guide*, Andrew D. Lester suggests a process to help us. He advises us to be alert for those occasions when we're angry and to stop and realize these feelings are the result of being anxious. Then we need to remember that anxiety is the result of being threatened. Therefore, the obvious course of action is to identify the threat.

Lester points out that we can use the same process of reasoning to understand other people's anger. For example, your daughter Angela is angry. So she must have some anxiety or other. You ask yourself, what threat to her or to someone around her is causing that anxiety? In this way, you see anger as the ultimate symptom of some event or issue that needs to be confronted. Put the focus where it needs to be put so that you'll be able to take responsibility for dealing with the anger "more creatively and ethically."[1] When you consider the situation this carefully, you realize we're making Angela's temper tantrums the issue, when what you really need to deal with is her confusion about a new baby in the house, or some other issue that simply needs to be identified.

The Values of Anger

When I am angry I can write, pray, and preach well, for then my whole temperament is quickened, my understanding sharpened, and all mundane vexations and temptations gone.
—Martin Luther

Anger can be useful and God-given, but the expression of it is another issue entirely. We need to underline the difference between those two.

Everyone feels angry, but that's only the beginning of the story. How will we handle our anger? The Bible says, "In your anger do not sin." Thus the anger and the sin are separate issues, and sin is any inappropriate response to the condition. Anger isn't a sin but an opportunity that may lead us to do some good or some evil. We'll consider in this book many damaging forms of anger expression, but for now let's explore the values of anger.

As we all know, one's self-concept is a very significant issue. We all need enough emotional and mental space to express who we are and what we can do. We all need some degree of autonomy, appropriate to our age and responsibilities. We all need to know that we are loved by someone we value. We need all these things, but we struggle to find and to hold them all our lives. Self-concept remains a work in progress. And when any aspect of it is threatened, we feel anxious and ultimately angry.

Children are working on that self-concept, too. This is the process of "growing up," or reaching maturity—the pursuit to discover exactly who they are. They are not only discovering what they are about, but what the world is about as well. Those two great concerns, the self and the world, are inevitably going to bump into each other at some point.

The toddler self is curious; he is discovering who he is by exploring. He is discovering what the world is like by touching and handling. Some things—light sockets, tiny objects—are inappropriate for the toddler to handle at this fragile stage in life. When the toddler self and the world come into conflict, anger results. And the anger itself is not bad, because it helps the child confront important new truths and resolve where he stands in relation to them.

We have labeled some of the key periods in which our children want to express their individuality. We know about "the terrible twos." We are concerned about puberty as well as the rites of passage of young adults leaving the nest. At each of these well-known junctures, young people push toward independence and individuation. It's a bumpy journey at best; the whole path is beset by collisions, confrontations, and adjustments, always marked by normal anger. As a toddler, as a teen, as a twenty-something, the individual will reach for more than we think is wise at the moment: investigating the shiny ornament; going on the first date; starting a risky new business venture. There is frustration and anger, and our children are making various statements to us through their lives:

"Pay attention to me. I don't like what you are doing. Restore my pride. You're in my way. Danger. Give me justice."[2]

It makes a world of difference to know what the journey is about, to understand that it's not only normal but necessary for children to strive for a greater sense of self. When our children know that we understand their push for more space, freedom, and authority, we will find ourselves working together rather than against one another. They will see us as allies coming to their aid rather than enemies blocking their progress.

Anger is like a horse that can take us many new places when it is tamed, but can run wild if left to its own resources. Because someone is angry at death and disease, a miracle vaccine is discovered. Because someone is angry at poverty and injustice, social change is finally brought about. Because one is angry about his physical condition, he adjusts his diet and exercise. Because your son is angry about striking out in the little league game, he works to become a better hitter. He channels his anger into healthy growth and competence.

Anger mobilizes our reserves. It makes our blood pump and fills us with adrenaline. Many angry people release the adrenaline by slamming doors, rolling around on the floor in tantrums, or shouting at someone. There are better, healthier, and more creative ways to put our anger to use. To find them, we need the best information about who we are, what we want, and what is being threatened. Then, we can express our feelings and carefully channel them in the proper direction.

Marilyn, a wonderful social worker, provided me with a perfect example. She passed me in the hall one day, beaming from ear to ear. I couldn't help but stop her to find out what inspired such a pleasing smile. As I listened with interest, Marilyn began to tell me the story of Dot, a young mother of three. Dot had been physically abused by her husband for months. Finally, the young woman had taken counsel from a well-known Christian whose firm advice was for Dot to be "submissive" to her husband—regardless of his treatment. The abuse continued, and finally Dot's friends could stand it no longer. They brought her to the center, where she met Marilyn.

It became clear to Marilyn that Dot was an extremely dependent person, incapable of taking the critical steps to protect herself. The one thing that roused her to action was a threat of harm to her children. When the husband even hinted at a move in that direction, Dot was filled with anger and sudden energy. She was finally able to take action to get help and to protect her children as well as herself.

Anger is nature's life preserver. We all have the survival instinct that is triggered when danger beckons. To extraordinary lengths, we will do what it takes to survive. Anger actually sharpens our senses—inner and outer—and provides a heightened awareness that informs us on how to proceed in protecting ourselves. Watch a grazing deer who hears a twig snap. Watch a small animal's eyes when caught in the headlight of your car. We are never more aware, more alert, than when we sense danger.

The survival instinct drives us to find out what we're cut out for in life. Those devastated by divorce, for example, often enter periods of great self-discovery. In simply trying to survive life's tumult, they set out to discover exactly who they must now be if the old self-image as husband or wife has been snatched away. These survivors discover new gifts, new desires, and new hopes and dreams. One of the "silver linings" of life's dark clouds is that we become energetic, aware, and creative even in the face of life's tragedies.

Some divorced people, on the other hand, cling to their anger for astonishing periods of time. They are unable to use their emotional energy to forge a new life; instead, they let the anger remain focused on the past until they are burdened by bitterness.

What will we do with our anger? Find a cure for disease, or let the anger add to the devastation of the disease?

Anger's Classroom

Anger responses aren't always spontaneous, but rather may be learned behavior. We learn to be angry through the culture that surrounds us. This may be a distinct geographical region, a tribe of some kind, or a religious or ethnic identity. One of the distinctives of a particular cultural backdrop is the way its people are taught to express their anger.

The two genders can even be considered to be distinct cultures unto themselves. Men are sometimes allowed to express anger in certain ways that will be different than those of women. Psychologist Charles Spielberger of the University of South Florida notes that this holds true even for young adults, a group thought to hold traditional gender roles at arm's length. Young women will choke back or deny their anger just as their mothers do, because this is what life has taught them. More so than men, women crave peace and clear relationships, so we find that they are far more likely to make the sacrifice of repressing their anger.[3]

A family, too, is a tiny culture unto itself. Every home has its unique traditions, mores, and idiosyncrasies. Extended families have their own ways of speaking and reacting that have us smiling and remarking, "Just like a Smith," or, "All your cousins laugh just like that." We pass down a lot more than apple pie recipes through our families. We hand down perspectives, values, and approaches to anger. If Mom and Dad refuse to argue or confront their feelings, individually and as a couple, their children are likely to develop the same patterns of repression and suppression.

Meg Eastman calls these patterns the "dragons that inhabit families." Every family harbors a few unique dragons under its roof, and we tend to raise dragons that resemble the ones we grew up with. We start our own young families with the firm resolution that things will be different. We will not be as harsh as our fathers or as overreactive as our mothers. We want to avoid the unpleasant anger environments we grew up with. But despite our best efforts, we see those familiar dragons pushing their purple, spiked noses into the family room. How did this happen? Why is there the same kind and quantity of anger that we were certain we would avoid? Have we become our parents? No, we simply learned more from them than we ever realized.[4]

This doesn't have to be a negative experience. Children can watch and learn positive disciplines as well as negative ones. They may observe parents channeling anger into positive actions, to get to the true root of problems and to make family life better. They may observe you not retaliating but seeking to understand those who have done wrong, and they will learn that compassion is a powerful alternative to striking back in anger. If you let them see this kind of lifestyle, they will adopt it for their own lives, for it is much more attractive and desirable than living out the cycle of pain and retribution.

The family is a small cultural group, in fact the most powerful cultural group to which any of us belong. No other social influence is more powerful than the one beneath our roofs. It's so very important to monitor the growth and development of that cultural group. Listen to its language. Watch its behavior. Discover what your children are learning about love and life and anger as they live in this culture.

At times, you may laugh to see your children picking up pet expressions and mannerisms. But then you'll be disturbed to see them imitating the kind of behavior you don't admire in yourself. You may raise your voice and indulge in an outburst over something that seems significant—say, family debt or a wrecked car. Your daughter will follow your lead in reacting to smaller matters—a broken toy or the announcement of bedtime. You'd rather that she had learned about the object of your wrath, but what caught her attention was the wrath itself.

You can change the way your family interacts and expresses anger, but don't think it will be easy. Your family members won't necessarily appreciate your efforts to clean up the emotional environment. But stay the course. In the long run, you're making a substantial development in the adult character and integrity of the children you are raising.

Stop to recall the last angry outburst in your home. What was the issue? Who was involved? How was the crisis managed? What would you do differently now? It would be a useful exercise to take a few moments and write out your answers to these questions and also to resolve exactly how you'll handle matters next time.

POSITIVE

1. PLEASANT ● SEEKING RESOLUTION ● FOCUSING ANGER ON SOURCE ● HOLDING TO PRIMARY COMPLAINT ● THINKING LOGICALLY

2. PLEASANT ● FOCUSING ANGER ON SOURCE ● HOLDING TO PRIMARY COMPLAINT ● THINKING LOGICALLY

POSITIVE AND NEGATIVE

3. FOCUSING ANGER ON SOURCE ● HOLDING TO PRIMARY COMPLAINT ● THINKING LOGICALLY ● unpleasant, loud

4. HOLDING TO PRIMARY COMPLAINT ● THINKING LOGICALLY ● unpleasant, loud ● displacing anger to other sources

5. FOCUSING ANGER ON SOURCE ● HOLDING TO PRIMARY COMPLAINT ● THINKING LOGICALLY ● unpleasant, loud ● verbal abuse

6. THINKING LOGICALLY ● unpleasant, loud ● displacing anger to other sources ● expressing unrelated complaints

PRIMARILY NEGATIVE

7. unpleasant, loud ● displacing anger to other sources ● expressing unrelated complaints ● emotionally destructive behavior

8. unpleasant, loud ● displacing anger to other sources ● expressing unrelated complaints ● verbal abuse ● emotionally destructive behavior

9. unpleasant, loud ● cursing ● displacing anger to other sources ● expressing unrelated complaints ● verbal abuse ● emotionally destructive behavior

10. FOCUSING ANGER ON SOURCE ● unpleasant, loud ● cursing ● displacing anger to other sources ● throwing objects ● emotionally destructive behavior

11. unpleasant, loud ● cursing ● displacing anger to other sources ● throwing objects ● emotionally destructive behavior

NEGATIVE

12. FOCUSING ANGER ON SOURCE ● unpleasant, loud ● cursing ● destroying property ● verbal abuse ● emotionally destructive behavior

13. unpleasant, loud ● cursing ● displacing anger to other sources ● destroying property ● verbal abuse ● emotionally destructive behavior

14. unpleasant, loud ● cursing ● displacing anger to other sources ● destroying property ● verbal abuse ● physical abuse ● emotionally destructive behavior

15. passive-aggressive behavior

6

Passive, Yet Aggressive

Anger is a many-headed beast. We cast it upon the world verbally.
We act it out, with explosive suddenness or over a period of years.
We turn it completely inward to the point of self-destruction.
Which is the most dangerous of anger's faces? Which does the most
damage?

If I were to ask this question to the average man or woman on
the street, that person would most likely speak of some kind of
quick, temperamental flair of aggression. That's the image we have
of anger that bursts into flame and threatens to burn anyone or
anything in the immediate vicinity.

But the truth is that another form of angry expression is more
dangerous still. Anger that does not burst into flame but smolders
invisibly is the kind we call passive-aggressive anger. If you were to
throw a match onto a pile of brush and kindling, the flames would
rise quickly. But if you were to set a woolen sweater on fire, it
would smolder quietly, undetected, until the time was past for any
attempt to prevent the damage.

Passive-aggressive anger is a smoldering flame, and we will
examine it carefully in this chapter. To avoid many common misunderstandings about this term, we'll attempt to be precise in its
definition as we explore how it works within and around people.

One thing is certain: no one is completely devoid of passive-aggressive anger. We all deal with it, and we all succumb, at least to some extent. But some people are much more prone to this kind of hidden festering. They hold greater levels of unchanneled anger within, and their ultimate expressions of it carry much greater consequences. I believe we may well have more people with hidden, toxic anger levels walking the streets in our society than ever before.

Passive-aggressive behavior is certainly difficult to understand, and that may be why there are many mistaken assumptions about it. The very name seems to be an oxymoron—a contradiction in terms. If you think about it, the words seem to be saying "passive active," for to be aggressive is to move, to take action. Let's take a look at each of the two words and explore exactly how they fit together.

In their book, *Speaking the Truth in Love: How to Be an Assertive Christian*, Ruth N. Koch and Kenneth C. Haugk help us to define passive aggression. They explain that the word passive means "not acting," but it also comes from a Latin word meaning "to suffer." In other words, here is a person who is refraining from action yet enduring some kind of pain. And why is the person passive? He or she places great stock in the feelings of others and wants to avoid bringing about disapproval by speaking up. So the person is crying on the inside, as the old cliche has it.

Aggressive, Koch and Haugk explain, is behavior that cuts against the grain, particularly in terms of other people. Aggressive people carry the assumption that they're entitled to act without regard to the other person's feelings, needs, or position. An aggressor doesn't restrain himself, but moves forcefully. However—key point—aggression is expressed not just in overt physical action but verbally, through body language, and in that specific brand of action (or inaction) we call passive aggression.[1]

Another way of examining these two terms is to say that passive people—"aggressively suffering"—act against themselves, while aggressive people act against others. But how are these two ideas linked in one person?

Koch and Haugk tell us that passive aggression is aggression through subtlety, a shrewd and secretive way of taking action to manipulate, circumvent, or triumph over someone else in order to achieve goals. These individuals refuse to speak or act in a straight-forward manner. They keep their own counsel and act on their own schedule.[2]

Therefore, we can define passive-aggressive behavior, but recognizing it is another matter entirely. Upon learning about this brand of behavior, we need to take care. There's a tendency to label every act of childish misbehavior as passive aggression, but that's a mistake. If we want to identify passive-aggressive behavior, we can begin by watching out for three distinctives:

- Passive aggression is irrational and illogical. Though we have said that such individuals act things out slowly and according to their own schedule, we're not talking about a carefully considered path of action. Instead, their actions are driven by the subconscious mind, where logic isn't the prime mover. The subconscious is driven by feelings, impressions, and powerful emotions. Passive-aggressive behavior is a nonimmediate reaction arising from anger, and therefore it is designed to run completely counter to what is expected—the opposite of what the person ought to do.

- Passive aggression's purpose as a reaction is primarily to upset the parents or other authority figures. We may try any strategy to correct the behavior, but it's not going to work. As a matter of fact, the more effort the parents put into curbing the behavior, the more determined will be the child's efforts to upset them. And because the actions are illogical and irrational, the parents almost always will be upset. This makes the passive-aggressive child feel successful, and he or she will step up efforts to cause even more frustration. The most common areas of combat in children are usually grades and values.

The opposite of passive aggression is calm, responsible and logical action—and this is what we as parents want for our children. Sometimes a parent-child conflict under these conditions is like one of those old-fashioned Chinese Finger Traps. In case you don't remember, that's the little flaxen cylinder with two openings for inserting a finger from each hand. When you try to pull your fingers out, of course, the flax tightens. The more you pull, the more hopeless your plight. You can only get free by relaxing and letting the flax do the same.

With passive aggression, pulling against the resistance only makes things worse. There will be no resolution for the time being; it's best to play the waiting game.

• Children ultimately hurt themselves the most by passive-aggressive behavior. They are focused on striking back at their parents, teachers, or other authority figures, but they are ultimately their own greatest victims. A fourth-grader may bring in the worst grades possible because he knows that low grades are guaranteed to upset his father. But he is the one who must live with the future that may result from low grades. Approximately one-third of college freshmen flunk out every year. The vast majority of these kids are perfectly capable of making decent grades. Could it be that many of these students are acting out their anger against someone without even realizing it?

Some individuals move into more serious kinds of passive-aggressive behavior through drugs, alcohol, disease, poverty, or even suicide, the ultimate passive-aggressive behavior. Remember, we are talking about illogical, irrational behavior.

The Roots of Passive Aggression

In chapter 5, we observed a few childish means of expressing anger. Every adult realizes the inappropriateness of these actions, but children do not. Why should they, when they haven't been trained to manage their anger effectively? They will naturally vent and act out their aggression. But parents, disturbed by these unpleasant displays, often will respond in ways that complicate the problem. Their reactions actually cause children to handle their anger in ways that are even more unattractive and inappropriate. But children will also handle their anger subconsciously, through passive aggression.

How many times have you and I observed a scene such as this? Judy is angry and snaps at her mother with great impudence. Her father overhears from the next room, puts down his newspaper, and says, "Don't you take that tone with your mother! I never want to hear you speak to your parents like that again! Do you understand?"

In that common scenario, Judy receives no guidance in how to deal with her anger. What she does learn is that certain words and tones of voice are unacceptable, that overt expressions of anger will get her into hot water, and that apparently the only course of action is to suppress her feelings. This is, of course, the open door to passive-aggressive anger.

Children are powerless. Judy's parents can defend themselves from her anger simply by demanding its suppression, but how can she defend herself from their anger? She knows that her parents can make her life miserable if she displeases them. If she were shown how to deal with her anger in a mature fashion, she could "keep it on the outside," where it could be rationally handled and channeled in a positive direction. Let me quickly add that "anger on the outside" doesn't mean the full and complete ventilation of emotions, but it does mean confronting the reasons for the anger.

Judy's parents, however, haven't provided her with any means to deal helpfully with her anger. Her only option is to bury it deep inside her. And as we have seen, the anger won't dissolve once it is buried like an organic substance; it's much more like toxic waste. It will spread in the soil of the self and ultimately find some new form in antiauthority attitudes, which will in turn become the seeds of passive aggression.

All of us suppress a certain amount of anger; normal social functioning dictates that. But when serious suppression of anger continues for years and rebellious attitudes survive into adulthood, the result is a dangerously passive-aggressive person. She has polished the skill of oversuppressing her anger, then releasing it in ways that are nearly impossible for others to deal with.

Consider the stories of Marge and Jane.

Marge

Marge's worried mother first brought the girl to my office. Marge was 19, blonde-haired, blue-eyed, and a very attractive young lady. Both of them were smiling and friendly as I stood to meet them. But they got right to business.

"Well, it's like this," Marge said. "Mom and Dad are upset about my engagement to Duane. You need to know, Dr. Campbell, that Duane is black. We met at college, and I love him. He is really wonderful. I just don't understand why my parents can't accept the man I've chosen."

Marge's mother, Ellen, quickly jumped into the conversation, a bit defensive. "We're not prejudiced, Dr. Campbell—just worried about our daughter. We worry about what this marriage will mean to Duane as well. And then there's the whole subject of children. We just don't want anyone to be hurt."

I was deeply impressed by the sincerity of both mother and daughter, and my heart ached for them.

"Tell me about Duane," I asked.

Marge's eyes lit up. "He's wonderful. He's smart, good-looking, sweet, kind, and he loves me."

"You're good at putting things in a nutshell," I kidded her, trying to lighten the tension that was building in the room.

Ellen admitted that what her daughter said was true. "Duane is certainly a fine boy, Dr. Campbell; there's no doubt about that. But being a good person is not enough. These kids need to face all the problems they're bound to have in the future."

I looked at Marge and asked, "What does your father say about this?"

The light immediately left Marge's eyes. She seemed to melt down into her chair. "He's totally against the marriage," she said a bit icily, "and he refuses to even talk about it." She looked up at me, now meaning business. "I'm going to marry Duane, and that's all there is to it. My marriage is my decision." I saw twin spots of rage reddening on Marge's cheeks.

A week later, I found myself sitting down for a meeting with Fred, Marge's father. He was a stern, relatively cold customer who spoke in rather abrasive tones and only when asked a direct question. During our time together, most of his remarks were complaints about his wife, his children, or his job. It was clear that Fred was a distressed and unhappy man. He was extremely angry about Marge's relationship with Duane and could find little good to say about either of them. My session with Fred left me sad and troubled.

Duane, on the other hand, was a pleasure to meet. He came in three days later. Marge had not been exaggerating his finer qualities; here was an impressive, outgoing young man who was instantly likeable. His deep love for Marge was crystal clear.

How could we resolve this impasse? I spent time conversing with all parties, and I administered some tests. The factor that stood out most was the deep rage that Marge felt toward her father. It was also obvious that she was handling her anger in passive-aggressive ways.

Over the next few weeks, Marge's work in school suffered. Once she had been a brilliant student, but now she decided to drop out of college. Meanwhile, the alteration in her behavior was damaging her relationship with Duane. She was behaving in passive-aggressive patterns toward him that left him hurt and confused. Marge lied about various subjects, and she secretly dated other boys. Needless to say, their engagement was a brief one.

It's possible to consider the case of Marge and come to the conclusion that, from the very beginning, she was acting unconsciously to hurt her father. It's not a question of how one feels about interracial or intercultural marriages—I've known people with wonderful experiences in that regard. Marge had simply found the particular trigger most likely to set her father off. I've observed many romances that seemed to have been sparked by subconscious intentions. After all, how better to hurt our parents than to marry someone who doesn't meet their approval?

But as we've seen, the greatest victims of passive-aggressive anger are the ones who harbor it. Marge brought terrible pain to her life, dropping out of college and harming many of her friendships as she descended into the spiral of irrational, angry behavior. A marriage to Duane would have brought pain to him and to any children who came from the union.

I can report a happy ending to this story, however. Through a lengthy period of counseling, Marge learned to handle her anger appropriately. In time, she was able to gain control over her passive-aggressive behavior and bring some equilibrium to her life.

Jane

Jane was one pale teenager as she entered my office. It was clear that she was nervous and not ready to speak freely, so I respected her feelings. We sat quietly for several minutes until she finally cleared her throat and meekly offered a few words. She expressed how difficult it was even for her to be here. Having gotten this far, Jane was still uncertain she'd be able to find the courage to reveal what was on her troubled mind.

We made a bit of small talk about school and hobbies until Jane suddenly unburdened herself of her secret. She was terribly confused about a homosexual encounter with a basketball teammate she "fell into" at college. Nothing like this had ever happened to her, and she didn't know what to think or feel about it.

I asked the girl about her parents. Jane told me her father was a successful businessman who was devoted to his wife. He was well respected in his community and church. Jane's mother was also a fine person, and Jane loved and respected both of them. However, I ascertained that both parents led fairly hectic, activity-filled lives that left little time for spending with their daughter. Oh, but the time they did spend together was "quality time," she assured me.

I also gathered that Jane's father had a bit of a temper. When Jane did something to make him angry, he really "unloaded" on her. Naturally, Jane tried very hard not to displease him and experience such wrath.

Testing and further interviews with Jane showed that she was a deeply depressed young woman who harbored a great deal of anger. The two primary causes of her anger: feeling unloved by her parents and her severe depression.

Jane's moods of depression were an irritant to her father. It was very important to spare him the truth of her emotional struggles. So she had learned to process her anger in a passive-aggressive manner, which ultimately led to her sexual response to her teammate. After she was treated for depression and could handle her anger in more direct and appropriate ways, she was better able to understand herself.

Jane was not a homosexual; rather, she was using passive-aggressive behavior to express her intense anger. Her situation is not an uncommon one.

Adults Are Passive-Aggressive, Too

I've mentioned my target age of 17 for developing mature character. Marge and Jane had both passed that age, but they still, through dedicated counseling and work, managed to overcome their passive-aggressive behavior. They were quite fortunate, because if their problems had extended into adulthood, the pain and damage would have escalated. As we move from childhood to adolescence to adulthood, our reach expands; we can bring about ever-greater turmoil for ourselves and others.

Two areas particularly susceptible to such havoc are work and marriage. Let's consider the effect on both.

Joe has been newly hired in a sales company. One of the assets not listed on his resume is a substantial supply of anger inside. But the human resources director, needless to say, only sees the bright and sunny side of Joe in job interviews. And for the first year or so, his antiauthority attitudes remain benign. He has begun work with a clean slate of feelings toward his boss. But as the weeks and months roll by, Joe will accumulate reasons for resentment, real or imagined, toward those above him on the corporate ladder. He will suppress his anger for as long as he can, but two years will probably be the limit.

Joe is unaware of the change, but lately he tends to do the opposite of what his supervisor wants him to do. As Paul described it in a moment of transparency, "I am ... a slave to sin. I do not understand what I do. For what I want to do I do not do, but what I hate I do" (Rom. 7:14–15). Joe's strange behavior, he realizes, cuts down on his sales commissions. It also makes his work relationships very uncomfortable. Yet he can't seem to break the cycle.

Those who work with Joe notice a gradual change of attitude. For two years, they would have described him as pleasant and cooperative, but more and more they would say he is difficult and annoying. The complaints come, and eventually Joe finds himself out of a good job he had been delighted to have.

Don't forget that the boss can be passive-aggressive, too. He's no less likely to be the one who is making life miserable for those beneath him.

What about Joe's home life? The damage caused by his anger will be just as severe.

Joe and Kathy dated for a year before marrying. Kathy has seen only the same bright and sunny young man that the human resources director has met. The couple spent countless hours together during their dating period, and Kathy is convinced she knows her fiancé well.

Since the wedding, life has been happy and hopeful. Joe enjoys planning the new house they hope to own, and he is very energetic in pursuing a good job with future possibilities. Kathy would never have any way of expecting the changes that are due—but the changes come.

At one time, the two seemed almost incapable of a prolonged argument; now, Joe almost seems to look for opportunities to create a dispute. He knows what little things are important to her, and he seems to do precisely the opposite—dirty clothing discarded on the floor, for example. Surely such a simple request wouldn't prove difficult for him to grant. Yet it seems as if, once she has mentioned her particular aversion to clothing on the floor, he begins to drop his things there more often.

You may wonder why a passive-aggressive individual would rebel against a spouse who isn't purely an authority figure. But authority figures include not only those to whom we are responsible, but also those for whom we are responsible.

Marriage to a passive-aggressive individual can resemble an ongoing nightmare with no escape, for the possibilities for upsetting the spouse are endless and reach into all areas of life. Common expressions of passive aggression in marriage are lying, physical and emotional rejection, generalized blame, mismanagement of money, and seething anger.

None of these expressions are exactly what people are looking for in a marriage commitment.

How Much Is "Normal"?

At one life stage, passive aggression actually could be considered "normal." In early adolescence, ages 13 to 15, children will typically adopt these patterns for handling their feelings. As long as their behavior hurts no one and causes no damage, we may consider this a "normal" stage.

And why not? We can all agree that it's quite difficult to be a teenager in today's world. There is no shortage of temptations or poor choices to make. There are more challenges within families with the rise of divorce rates. There is social confusion over matters such as sexual roles and ethical boundaries. There's plenty to be frustrated and angry about. As we've seen, the adolescent self is reaching out to develop its self-concept, as well as to understand a puzzling world. Passive-aggressive impulses can take damaging forms.

In simpler times, against a more rural backdrop, teenagers expended their excess energy by putting Farmer Brown's cow on top of the barn or overturning a few outhouses. When I was young, we took a friend's Volkswagen Beetle apart and reassembled it in his bedroom while he was away on vacation. By the time my own children were teens, I was grateful for the simpler adolescent antics: toilet-papering the yards of their friends, for example.

Today's world is much more complicated, much more loaded with dangerous possibilities. Drugs, guns, alcohol, and the like are available to children. Young people are bombarded with cultural expression—movies, television, and video games—that keeps their attention riveted on sex, violence, and despair. And all of this comes into a context of normal teenage depression.

The normal expressions of this behavior tend to start around 10 or 11 years of age, when the child begins neglecting ordinary chores, dawdling, or generally upsetting the parents. When parents know that such behavior is normal, they can handle it in a healthy manner, even though it is irritating and likely to continue for several years.

If parents deal effectively with their children's behavior, that behavior is less likely to extend outside the home. On the other hand, if the parents do a poor job helping their children in this regard, the passive-aggressive behavior will spread outward to school, neighborhood, church. We need to deal squarely and wisely with the annoyances right at the source—under our roofs.

Does your child's messy room irritate you? That's to be expected, but try to remember that angrier, more passive-aggressive expressions would be less preferable alternatives. If your child limits his angry behavior to messiness, dawdling, noise, and unkempt appearance, then your situation will at least be manageable. Family life may take a bit of extra work, but nothing there would indicate your child will not emerge as a young adult with integrity and strong character. Help your child manage those "trace amounts" of anger; keep it from being buried within, and you'll avoid the perilous paths of Marge and Jane.

Remember this: In the full throes of adolescence, your children will behave in more extreme ways. They'll choose the clothing that is bound to start an argument. They'll clam up on the subjects they see you're anxious to discuss with them. They'll gravitate toward the friends you've expressed uncertainty about. In other words, they'll go for the jugular, and you'll feel they've dedicated their young lives to driving you crazy.

If your family is devout in spiritual beliefs, you can expect your adolescent to choose that battlefield as well. If you place a great premium on his Sunday school attendance or youth group participation, you're going to hear, "I don't want to go to church today." You'll be puzzled, because you know your child's best friends are there.

Will you overreact in anger? If so, you may entrench the rebellion so deeply that, in later years, your child will have been driven away from God permanently. In many cases, grown children consciously and angrily reject the faith of their fathers. What we discover is that the issue is almost never the faith, but the fathers. Still, remember that the rebellion is not ultimately directed at you or God, but is a normal stage of adolescence to handle carefully and compassionately.

Another important battleground is the classroom. Every child knows her parents care deeply about grades, so it's not surprising when our children use their report cards as weapons of rebellion. Falling grades will upset Mom and Dad every time. If you can avoid overreaction and be conscious of this area as just another aspect of the age and stage, your kids will return to the right path more quickly and with fewer unpleasant confrontations.

At the beginning of this book, we defined integrity. An important element of it, we agreed, was for one to take responsibility for personal behavior. The passive aggressor refuses to take responsibility, but pushes it toward parents, teachers, or someone else. Mom will be tempted to do her daughter's homework for her; Dad will find himself taking over writing his son's essay. You must refuse to be manipulated in this direction. Instead, insist that your child take responsibility. You may have to grit your teeth and weather a few Ds and Fs to teach that lesson.

You may recognize the following phenomenon if you've had a fifth-grader in your home recently. Kids this age will begin to "forget" their homework. The assignment isn't turned in, and the teacher sends a note home to the parents: "You need to know that Freddy hasn't been turning in his homework." The parents then become obsessed with checking to make sure textbooks and assignments come in the door. End of problem? No, because now Freddy "forgets" to take the homework assignment back to school. When Mom and Dad add that to their daily checklist, the children "forget" to take the work from their desks and hand it to the teacher.

I remember going to my son's classroom during Open House night and seeing all the fifth grade homework stashed away in desks. It's as predictable as clockwork.

Of course, fifth grade isn't the only challenging milestone. When my older son, David, was in eighth grade, his grades slid from As and Bs to Cs. I knew that this was fairly normal, so I made certain not to overreact. I kept an eye on the matter but let David know that good grades were his responsibility.

By the time he was in tenth grade, however, he was still struggling along. Just as I was really beginning to perspire, David woke up. It occurred to him that his older friends were all heading for fine colleges, and he was going to be left behind. When David finally came to me to talk about his future, I felt free to share my concerns. I knew he would hear me now because he was interested in making better grades.

David wanted to know what grade-point average would get him into a good school. I showed him the catalog from the college his sister was attending. My son studied the information and frowned. "Looks like I have my work cut out for me," he said somberly.

Needless to say, David's grades quickly spiraled upward because he was determined to get the job done. In the end, no amount of ranting or raving from his mother or me would have improved his grades; he had to do it himself. And if we had entrenched the battle lines and raised the angry rhetoric, he might well never have made it to his high school diploma.

Dealing with a Normal Level

We call a certain level of teenage passive-aggressive behavior "normal." But at the time, it certainly doesn't feel very normal. These parenting episodes bring us headaches and lost sleep. But at all costs, we must avoid the tendency to become the provokers after we've been provoked. Our own levels of internal anger begin to build up, and our kids see our eyes when we look at them and they hear our tones when we speak to them.

Children struggle with the tremendous burden of emotional growing pains, and they cannot take on the additional burden of their parents' anger. They have no safeguards, and our anger will bring about damage inside their fragile psyches.

How do we speak when we are angry? We tend to drop to a tone of voice that is lower on the melodic scale. Anticipating an argument or resistance, Mom will say, "I want you to empty the garbage now," with a lower inflection at the end. No one enjoys being spoken to in such tones, and children become angry. If they feel themselves to be powerless targets of anger, they will begin to behave in passive-aggressive patterns.

Here are some very practical points about demeanor during a parent-child conflict:

- Let Yogi Bear be your model for tone of voice! Can you remember that character's speech patterns? He invariably ends every sentence with an upward inflection. His comments start low and end high. When you talk to your children, this approach will make your words inviting rather than threatening. They'll help deflect anger.

- Try to avoid phrasing your sentences as commands: "Go do your homework immediately." Cold commands, of course, can seem depersonalizing or disempowering to children who are trying to form a self-concept. Instead, it makes sense to replace the imperative tense with the interrogative tense: "You think it might be a good idea to get on that homework?" Instead of Yogi Bear, you can use the game show "Jeopardy" as your model: phrase everything in the form of a question.

- Keep the anger out of your eyes. We all know how we feel when we receive a "dirty look" from a child or a co-worker. But sometimes people don't realize what their eyes are saying. Parents often fail to realize they're "looking daggers" at their kids. Looking away from the child sends a subtle message of nonacceptance as well. As difficult as it may be, we need to maintain eye contact—loving eye contact, not a glare.

- Loving eye contact doesn't mean smiling or laughing—those are actually poor strategies. Some adults lapse into these as nervous habits when they are tense. But just as laughter draws us together when we're on good terms, it distances us when we're not. Don't let your child draw the wrong conclusion that you don't take her seriously, or that you're ridiculing her.

- Work on cultivating the neutral look. This takes a little work, so you'll want to practice in front of a mirror. Don't feel foolish, but remember your demeanor is critically important in your relationship with your children. If you naturally smile or frown much of the time, just by habit, you might be causing communication problems you don't even suspect.

Does it sound as if I am trying to prepare you for your child's angry moments? That's exactly what I'm doing. It helps to be prepared for the most annoying, frustrating, and totally upsetting moments of parenthood. These episodes bring out the worst in us—in our faces, our voices, and our behavior. It will take plenty of self-discipline to control our own anger so we can help our children learn to control theirs. Think about how you (not just your child) would appear if someone were videotaping your confrontation. Consider how you might feel if you were in your child's shoes.

When you are faced with an angry child, you have two obligations—to accept your child's anger, ugly as it is, and to control your own anger, ugly as it may want to be. I know this is difficult, but it is critical when you think of your goal—that your child will be continually learning to handle anger in a more mature manner. You will be your child's model, for good or for worse. Meet your child's anger and deal with it positively so it won't be buried deep within a changing, developing young person only to resurface as passive-aggressive behavior. Then you will see your child emerge from the normal passive-aggressive stage at around that age of 17—one of the greatest blessings and triumphs of parenting.

Ascending the Anger Ladder

I'm sure you saw the Anger Ladder in chapter 5. As you work with your children in the coming years, you will always be seeking to help them climb from one rung to the next, leaving the negative expressions behind as they reach upward for the more positive ones. This is a long process that involves both training and example.

You'll notice that passive aggression is at the bottom of the Ladder. Whether you have 30 rungs or 60, passive-aggressive expressions of anger will always be at the bottom. It's the worst of all options, yet it is common to teenagers. You'll have to meet your child on that bottom rung, but the important thing is not staying there.

Be ready to help with the climb, but remember that your child can handle only one rung at a time. Naturally, we're in a hurry to reach the top, to arrive at a place of pleasant maturity. The hard part is waiting for children to be ready, on their own schedules, to take that next step. This will call upon our greatest reserves of patience and wisdom. But I can tell you that the results are well worth the wait. Pat and I have seen our children move to mature expressions of anger as we let them grow at their own pace. Carefully observe your child's expressions of anger; you'll be able to identify his place on the Ladder and think about the next step.

I remember the most uncomfortable step on that ladder, when David was about 13. He was really putting on a demonstration on the use of the poison tongue. I can only be grateful that this stage didn't last very long. I was the target of his verbal anger, and it was difficult for me to endure without snapping back. I had to make use of some self-talk to determine where he was on the Anger Ladder. I would say to myself, "Attaboy, David, Attaboy. Let that anger out—because when it's all out, I've got you!" Of course, I didn't say any of those words aloud. All I was doing was silently reinforcing my own patience.

Was I right in allowing my son to let his anger out freely? I knew that as long as it was trapped inside him, it would control and dominate our home. Once he brought it to the outside, he could hear himself—and he felt silly. When a small child is afraid of something dark peering from the doorway of his bedroom at night, how do we help her deal with her fear? We turn on the light, open the door wide, and let the light shine on the object that is frightening her. Then she sees for herself that the monster is nothing more than a familiar old coat whose sleeve was protruding. Light puts things in their perspective; cramming things into the darkness makes them into monsters.

As soon as I let my son see his own behavior in a revealing light, I could regain control. He had gotten all the anger out verbally and was ready to be sensible. "Now what do I do?" he could ask, and this was my invitation to use the moment for training. The tirade became the teachable moment.

I also knew that every bit of fresh anger that poured from his mouth right now would no longer be there to emerge much later in the form of lying, stealing, sex, drugs, or anything worse. Better to nip it in the bud than let it grow into passive-aggressive anger.

This is a difficult subject, isn't it? Even now, you may have many questions you'd like to ask. It may be hard for you to imagine allowing a child to express his anger, because you weren't raised that way. Your parents wouldn't put up with temperamental outbursts, and their own parents were stricter still.

But allowing that anger is not the same as being permissive. We must remind ourselves over and over again that anger is inevitable. We cannot make it go away simply by forcing our children to hide it. And we certainly can't teach them a lesson in behavior by giving in to anger ourselves. We need to respect the power of the anger, knowing that its currently manageable portion now will take an unmanageable form at some point in the future.

In the end, this is the only way to teach our children that the best way for them to express their anger is verbally and pleasantly. If we don't let them speak, we're actually pushing their anger away where it can't be managed and can't be used as a teaching opportunity, and where it is certain to find an outlet in behavior.

But you may wonder about this issue of respect. Are your children being disrespectful when they show their anger? Not necessarily. If you'll think about your child's usual attitude toward your authority, you're likely to discover that your child has plenty of respect. Most children do. Anger is not about respect, but is a separate issue. We want to teach our children to say what they mean, to express themselves honestly, and to live with integrity.

When you become exasperated in trying to survive your children's anger, remember the tools in your arsenal. The Yogi Bear inflection is on your side. So is eye contact, the neutral demeanor, and, when all else fails, the silent encouragement of self-talk. This little storm will pass, too, and when your child's anger is spent, you're ready to communicate and to teach. That will be the subject of chapter 9. For now, remember that not only is your child going to grow through the expression of his anger; you, too, are going to grow through the restraint of your own.

We should also stop to acknowledge those children who seem to verbalize anger even when nothing has set them off. These children may be using their behavior to manipulate their parents, and that's a completely different matter. We're speaking of tantrums that are staged to force weary parents to give in on some desired objective of the child. That's a behavior you must recognize and correct—but the same rules apply. Your anger won't send the right message or help the situation. You need to be calm, pleasant, but also firm in your principles.

When your children bring their anger to parents, they are also bringing themselves to be trained. It is crucial not to begin training your child until both of you have calmed down and reestablished a good feeling between you. It is also crucial to avoid waiting too long, or you will lose the effect of building on what happened. Timing is critical. As soon as stability has been established between you, sit down together and do three things.

- You want to let your child know that you are not going to condemn. Especially if a child is very responsive to authority, the child may feel guilty about what he or she has done. Part of training is letting your child know that you accept him or her as a person and always want to know how your child is feeling, whether happy or sad or angry. I told David, "When you are angry, I want to know that you are."

- Next, you want to commend your child for the things he or she did right. I told David, "You did let me know that you were angry, and that is good. You didn't let your anger out on your little brother or the dog. You didn't throw anything or hit the wall. You simply told me that you were angry."

  Do you see where I am going with this? I looked for any occasion for praise, anything worthy of lifting up. Any time a child brings verbal anger to you, he or she has done some right things and avoided some wrong ones. By emphasizing the positive, you keep your child focused on that climb up the Anger Ladder—always reaching for the next rung. "If you didn't take it out on the dog this time, Son, then next time I know you can do even better."

- Finally, you want to do what we've just mentioned: help your child reach that next rung on the ladder. This involves giving a request rather than a prohibition. Instead of saying, "Don't ever call me that name again!" you say, "From now on, Son, I hope you won't call me that name. All right?" This, of course, provides no guarantee of obedience. A strong threat might actually be more likely to change immediate behavior. But your question gives your child the freedom and encouragement to strive for maturity independently—the only way it can be attained. He or she will take that step. It may be the next day or several weeks or months down the road. But you can't take that step for your child. You can only point the way and avoid complicating matters, using love rather than power.

After you have gone through the process enough times, your child will begin to do some thinking without your reminders. The combination of your training plus your good example of handling anger in a mature way will help your child to do self-training after a while.

Let's conclude this chapter by repeating that the very heart of this process is the unconditional love you want to give your children. When they see you ride out the storm, take the harsh words with grace, and refuse to withdraw your love and support when they're at their weakest and worst, they will see it. They will hear it. They will feel it.

Your children will securely know that they are truly loved, and in love we find the inner strength to keep moving onward and upward in the lifelong journey of becoming all that God means us to be.

7

The Lower Rungs of the Ladder

There is nothing passive-aggressive about Leona. She is 16, going through all the normal changes of adolescence, and she was born with high spirits. A quiet evening around the dinner table may suddenly erupt into shouted words of anger from Leona, in the blink of an eyelash—or a temper. Her mom may offer a meek question about how Leona is wearing her hair, and suddenly Leona opens an incoming barrage of verbal gunfire. When her mother leaves the room in tears, Leona feels guilty.

She is nothing like Ernie, her older brother, who kept to himself during his teenage years. When there was something wrong, you didn't hear him; then you didn't see him. The bedroom door would softly close.

Then there is Jerome, their cousin, who bullies younger kids at school. He isn't angry at those kids—he's angry at a host of other things. But he takes it out on three or four weaklings on the school bus who are easy prey.

We come into the world with a burden to bear. Anger is no "factory option" for the human machine but standard equipment on the human race. As we have seen, this is not completely a bad thing. But we all face the task of learning how to direct and dispense our personal allotment of anger. One person's anger creates a cure for polio; the other's anger sets off a world war.

Ideally, we will make the long, uphill struggle from anger's most immature and explosive forms to those marking the wise, well-adjusted adult. Few of us reach the top rungs of the Anger Ladder; many adults never climb more than a few rungs high. Passive-aggressive anger, the worst option of all, is rampant in the adult world we inhabit. Many parents are teaching their children the lessons of personal self-destruction without even realizing it. Passive aggression alone is a terribly serious issue, well worth a book—or a shelf of them.

But other dangers lurk in the lower regions of emotional expression. Let's examine a few destructive expressions of anger.

Aggression

Aggression is all about seeking to harm. The target may be another person, a group of people, or an object. The expression may take physical or verbal form. Acts of aggression may be crude or relatively sophisticated—the pen, it has been said, is mightier than the sword.

A child's aggression will be overt. She may attack by throwing a toy, shouting a protest, or hitting, biting, or scratching. She may do all of these things. But however, whenever, and to whomever aggression is expressed, it is always inappropriate. It always causes pain. It always leaves a trail of damage to relationships. Whatever the goal of the aggression may have been, it will be overshadowed by the pain that is sure to be experienced all around.

Many parents, of course, behave aggressively toward their children. They may feel this is their right, and they may feel it is even beneficial. But they should realize the certainty that their children ultimately will rebel against them. They should also realize that children will learn and imitate their parents' methods for dispensing anger.

Aggressive actions lurk toward the bottom of our Anger Ladder. They are complicated by their frequent combination with other destructive behaviors. And these actions usually are not isolated events but part of a chain that began aggressively somewhere in the past and will lead to more of the same—or worse—in the future.

Violence, as we know, begets violence. A child who observes violence, whether in person or on a television screen, is more likely to resort to violence himself. Dr. Leonard D. Eron, a professor of psychology at Yale University, spent two decades studying the causes of aggression in children. He came up with two conclusions:

• Children who watched more television expressed more aggression.
• The more television children watched, the more likely they were to commit aggressive crimes as adults.

Dr. Eron was convinced of his conclusion after 20 years of careful research. Indeed, when he revisited the children as they reached the age of 30, his findings were more conclusively proven than ever. Here were adult lives sadly devastated by anger.[1]

Our immediate reaction is to throw all the blame on those evil people who produce our movies and TV shows. A convenient scapegoat would make life very simple, wouldn't it? Simply unplug the set, throw it out the window, and you could expect your children to become placid and reasonable.

Life, of course, is never that simple. The problem of rampant aggression runs much deeper than any single contributing factor. I happen to believe that the leading predictor of future anger is the degree of antiauthority bias in a child's makeup—the level of passive aggression underlying the anger. Some of us are simply more prone to passive-aggressive reactions than others.

As we've seen, there is a difference between aggression and assertiveness. Assertive behavior is usually healthy and appropriate. Some people are more direct in their expression of feelings, anger included. This is a good thing, and assertiveness is one mark of a happy and successful adult life. When the intent to harm enters the equation, however, we've crossed over the line into aggression.

In *Taming the Dragon in Your Child*, Meg Eastman offers a number of helpful suggestions. She details specific behaviors such as fighting, blaming, and power struggles and concludes that many factors lead to children being aggressive and out of control. Stress may be the driving issue. Overactivity is a problem for many children. Abuse certainly would contribute. Or aggression could simply be a matter of parents failing to teach their children how to control themselves. Eastman points out that we often ignore aggression in young children. "They'll grow out of it," say comforting friends. But by school age, the patterns of anger haven't been left behind. They've become pronounced and more disturbing.

Perhaps the children crave a sense of control. Outbursts tend to accomplish that goal. Afterward, we notice the child's lack of remorse, even the tendency to blame others. The single key factor is the child's inability or unwillingness to accept responsibility for his or her actions.

What are the triggers for anger-based aggression in a child? Eastman offers these three kinds of events:

• Anything that threatens to lower a child's sense of status and control.
• Being exposed as a failure in class, on a team, or within the family or peer group.
• Challenges to the child's power base—not being given his way, being forced to follow a rule or to complete some assignment.[2]

Meg Eastman believes in drawing clear boundaries. She writes that the aggressive child needs "limits, limits, and more limits!" *Taming the Dragon in Your Child* would be worthy of close reading if aggression is a particular problem in your home.

Ventilation

The verbal expression of anger is ventilation—the behavior popularly called "venting." How is this different than, say, Leona's barrage of angry words? The aggressive tongue intends harm. It goes for the jugular. But venting is simply a way of ventilating or draining away the anger. It could be loud at times. It could be tediously "whiny" or a string of mumbled expletives. These days, people come to us and say, "I need to vent." We do our best to provide an understanding ear. But real venting, which includes the presence of anger, is unpleasant and disruptive for any of us to be around. We want our children to outgrow this phase by the time they are 17.

Still, we must recognize that as much as we dislike a child's venting, it does serve a purpose in childhood. It presents parents with a "teachable moment," an occasion for training children to understand and positively handle their anger. Venting is verbal, and the words raise a subject that we as parents can use. We also realize that if our children are talking about it, they aren't acting upon it. They aren't expressing their anger through behavior (aggression, passive aggression) and that's a good thing. Anger is going to emerge either physically or verbally, and if we must have anger (as we must), we would always choose a verbal expression. So when we're confronted with venting, we need to take the attitude that it could be worse—and it could be better if we seize the moment to train children.

When we "seal the vent"—in other words, silence our children as they try to express their anger—we push them toward an unwanted behavioral response. We need to catch ourselves before we shout, "Shut up!" or "I don't want to hear about it!" We don't want to hear about it, but they need us to. An ounce of prevention at the verbal stage is worth a pound of cure at the behavioral level.

Venting is unpleasant, but so are many chores we must face. It's crucial to be aware of the positive use parents can make of children's anger.

Nagging and Withholding

We all know about nagging. We have nagging headaches, nagging doubts, and nagging spouses. As far as people are concerned, nagging is an immature expression of anger that is closely related to ventilation. It's not a form of venting, however, because there are differences. Venting seeks to get rid of anger. Nagging is an activity we take up when we feel ineffective or powerless. We can't get someone else to do what we'd like the person to do. Billy wants to go to the new park with the high sliding board, but he has no means of getting there without a parent driving him. He feels powerless. So he nags his mom constantly to take him to the park.

But parents nag, too. We want our kids to eat vegetables. We want them to get their homework done as soon as they come home from school. We want them to clean their rooms. We don't want to have a loud confrontation, so we nag them. Nagging is a kind of sneaky or furtively expressed anger. It is a subtle way of dumping anger on a child. If we don't like being nagged, we have to imagine how children—who are forced to listen to their parents—feel about it. If we're not careful, our nagging will create a constant undercurrent of frustration that will push them toward antiauthority attitudes.

What about withholding? Sometimes we withhold dessert or that trip to the park as a very legitimate means of discipline. Every parent has to withhold certain things at certain times. But we need to make a close inspection of our own feelings. Are we punishing in a spirit of anger? Are we frustrated to the point that we punish simply to hurt the child? Many parents don't realize their own levels of anger laser focused on their children, and they also fail to realize that their children are well aware of it. Withholding as "payback" is a very bad and dangerous idea.

An angry parent may also withhold affection and nurture: "I'm not very happy with you today," we coldly say as we disappear behind the newspaper or book. We speak in formal tones and break eye contact. This is particularly dangerous because we are telling the child she isn't loved and because we're teaching an ominous lesson. We're showing children how to withhold affection, obedience, achievement, cooperation, pleasantness, or anything that might hurt their parents.

Silence and Withdrawal

Leona's brother Ernie practiced both silence and withdrawal. Many parents actually accept this behavior because it is more peaceful. But both of these are inappropriate and harmful in their own ways. Many adults are familiar with silence and withdrawal in the context of marriage, where relationships are seriously damaged by a growing refusal to communicate.

Sometimes these two expressions are simply ways to avoid admitting our anger and confronting a painful situation. As we all know, "confrontive" personalities seem to take conflicts and other relationships head on. The "nonconfrontive" types will go to any length to avoid dealing directly with any unpleasant issue. They choose tidy loneliness over messy honesty.

Don't be alarmed if you recognize yourself here! The common reluctance to risk an unpleasant argument isn't necessarily the same as withholding, though there is a close relationship. The key factor in silence and withdrawal is that we shut ourselves off from the relationship. But generally we don't realize what we're doing. A mother with an angry and confused adolescent son may throw up her hands and say, "I give up trying to understand him!" And she may let up in her efforts to ask questions and learn more about her son's world. She isn't intentionally withdrawing her love, but that's the effect just the same—and it's a very dangerous effect.

Silence and withdrawal are the opposite of unconditional love. To withdraw from the parent-child relationship is the same as telling the child, "Sometimes I love you, sometimes I don't." We are saying, "I would give you more love if you behaved more pleasantly. I would pay more attention to you if it didn't bother me so much." Yes, it's hard and often painful to be a parent, and at some stages our children don't seem to make it any easier. But when they observe conditional love, they become angry. The rage builds.

In marriages, too, we create a powerful anger when we turn away from each other. Divorce scenarios often startle the families, the friends, and the partners themselves. "I didn't know she was so angry!" he says. "Where did all that rage come from?" she says. It can't be heard because of silence; it can't be seen because of withdrawal.

We cannot afford to give in to these "bottom of the ladder" behaviors in marriage or parenting. If we do, we stoke the fires of rage and threaten to burn a relationship beyond recovery.

Writing from painful personal experience, Andrew D. Lester tells how he and his wife learned to deal with their anger constructively instead of retreating into silence. He explains that the couple decided to stop being afraid of their anger. They would take some risks; they would share the anger with each other, just as if it were any other thought or feeling. The two of them found themselves taking more responsibility for how their anger was expressed. They focused on using it constructively instead of stifling it and allowing it to spread as a cancer to a healthy relationship. Lester's conclusion: Anger actually increases intimacy when we deal with it honestly.[3]

Displaced Anger

What could be more puzzling than displaced anger? It seems to come from nowhere and have nothing to do with the time or place. This is anger "to go," taken from its place of origin and dumped somewhere else entirely. Perhaps a parent is the source, but a classmate is the target; Jerome, from the beginning of the chapter, practices displaced anger as he bullies weaker children on the school bus. The real targets of his anger are out of reach, so he must use the smaller children as surrogates.

What causes this behavior? Usually we're prevented from confronting the real target. We wouldn't dare say what we think to the boss at work. We may have fantasized an entire raging speech for the history teacher at school, but we don't want to be expelled. And quite frequently, parents have the most power to keep the truth from being aired. But the anger has to go somewhere, and it is inflicted on someone who has no idea why he or she is being attacked.

Sadly, often children become the targets for displaced anger. This is a complicating factor in the already confusing maze of parenting. A child will behave immaturely, and Dad, who has been verbally abused by his boss, dumps his reservoir of hostility on the child. The old cliche has it that the king kicks the duke, the duke kicks the baron, the baron kicks the peasant, the peasant kicks the wife, the wife kicks the child, and the child kicks the dog—and the dog bites the next person who walks by. Life can be an ugly cycle of displaced anger.

It is crucial to remember that children cannot tolerate parental anger because they have no defenses against it. Dumping any anger on them is harmful, but dumping excess rage from other sources can be truly destructive. When parents learn to control themselves, positive control of children's development will naturally follow.

Oversuppressed Anger vs. Ventilation

What about suppressing anger? That seems a simple enough question to many people, and perhaps that's why there are so many myths and misunderstandings about it today.

You've surely encountered the idea that it's unhealthy to bottle up feelings, that emotions must be vented on the spot. In the 1960s and 1970s, an era when the expression "let it all hang out" was in vogue, we heard a good deal on the subject. Theodore Rubin's *The Anger Book* is still on the bookshelves with its pro-venting view, and we take it for granted when a friend comes to us and says, "I need to vent."

It's true that overly suppressing anger may contribute to psychiatric illness, passive-aggressive behavior, and other problems. Genuine physical illness can even be triggered by anger that is tightly suppressed. Howard Friedman and Stephanie Booth-Kersley have observed that the following emotions have linked to physical disorders: anger, depression, hostility, anxiety, and introversion. And some of the illnesses, according to the same research, are heart disease, ulcers, headaches, arthritis, and asthma.[4]

However, simple ventilation of anger does not alleviate or prevent these problems. In fact, ventilation as a means of draining anger cannot only cause the problems but may also increase levels of rage. In all too many cases, it is like throwing gasoline on a fire.

Because the case for ventilation has been so publicized in psychological circles, I want to underscore it further. To say that "getting it out of your system" is completely beneficial is to ignore the surroundings and the consequences of angry expression. There is more to the subject than how we feel after venting. You may let it all hang out, get it all off your chest, tell it like it is, clear the air, and vent until there's nothing left to vent. As one writer has said, if your shocked listener shoots you on the spot, "it won't matter that you die with very healthy arteries."[5]

Carol Travis offers us three myths of expressed anger in *Anger: the Misunderstood Emotion*:

1. That aggression is the natural, instinctive way to work out anger (what we call catharsis).
2. Anger can be worked out or decreased simply by talking it out.
3. Tantrums and other childish expressions are healthy; they help us avoid neurosis.[6]

In brief, the author counters Myth #1 by pointing out that when children are permitted to play aggressively, they don't "work anything out." They become even more aggressive.[7]

In regards to the second myth, she argues that talking out our anger doesn't reduce it but revisits it. It maintains an attitude of hostility. This is true of all ages, as borne out by one particular test: Children who were allowed to express their anger toward another child ended up liking their antagonist even less than did the children who were restrained from expressing their anger.[8]

As for tantrums being healthy preventive maintenance for our neuroses, Carol Travis points out that parents fail to see the difference between angry expression and acts of aggression. They're worried about stifling their child's expressions of anger, so they allow all kinds of damaging and unrestrained displays. This only increases the child's aggressiveness.[9] Expression can be allowed without acting out aggression.

Self-Abuse

More and more people today follow the trend of pointing the finger of blame at someone else for their own problems—it's society's fault, it's my parent's fault, it's the stress I've had to manage this week. But there are still many who take the opposite strategy, blaming themselves when things go wrong.

They engage in negative self-talk: "I'm no good; it figures this would happen to me; I don't deserve any better." It's amazing how deeply some people can descend into the pits of self-blame and false guilt.

Turned inward, these emotions don't feel like anger so much as pain and hurt. All of life comes to have the theme of one's own personal punishment. Despair, depression, and feelings of helplessness and hopelessness build up. Depression is a major source of anger, and it's not surprising that we can find ourselves caught up in a destructive cycle of self-abuse.

Consider Betty, an account manager who has been dating Justin, a co-worker. She has begun to think about marriage, but she sees the relationship slipping away. No matter how hard she tries, she can't seem to make Justin take the relationship as seriously as she does. She feels out of control. Life is frustrating when we feel powerless to reach out and take the things we most desire. Betty begins to blame herself—why, it must have been her fault. Maybe if she had behaved this way or that way on her dates with Justin; maybe if she had learned to cook the dishes he likes; maybe, maybe, maybe. Who can she blame but herself?

Why would Betty think this way while another young lady might have blamed Justin or simply accepted the disappointment and moved on? The reasons for our differing responses are complex. In some ways, simple genetics make us unique. Some people keep their anger inside more than others. Some are more prone to melancholy or chemical depression.

Whatever the reasons, it is true that we're likely to train our children to handle anger as we do, and they may indeed share our genetic dispositions anyway. Are you a self-blamer? Do you store your anger deep inside? To what extent have you passed on these traits to your children? It is destructive to handle anger by either blaming ourselves or by blaming someone else.

Let's also realize that passive-aggressive attitudes aggravate self-abuse. Betty is now spending hours conversing with Justin as the relationship is clearly reaching its end. There are many things she'd like to say—angry thoughts about Justin that occur to her—but she still clings to the hope that she can somehow rescue the relationship. So she cannot express her anger in any way. This oversuppression will surely become passive-aggressive behavior. In time, she will have a desire for revenge—maybe even suicidal thoughts and attempts. Suicide is the ultimate passive-aggressive act: "He'll be sorry when I'm gone!"

We've spent considerable time now on the bottom rungs of the Anger Ladder. We could identify other inappropriate tactics, but most of those others are related to the ones we've discussed.

It is clear that we're not talking about a domain reserved for children. Many adults use these misguided, destructive approaches to anger. Perhaps you've recognized yourself at times. If so, you'll want to work on your own management of anger so you don't pass the wrong techniques on to your children.

Jesus quoted an old proverb from his time: "Physician, heal thyself" (Luke 4:23). We'll turn our attention now toward the needs of parents to do exactly that.

8

Starting with the Face in the Mirror

As we raise children, we want them to have the right friends. We worry about them drifting into the wrong crowds, picking up the wrong language and values. We worry about the television shows they soak in. We're concerned about what they learn at school, what they see on the Internet, and what they hear on their portable stereos.

But the truth, like it or not, is that parents have the greatest influence of all. Among all the contributors to their growth and development, we are the ones who make or break children. If you imagine a pie chart assigning the proper influence to all of these sources—friends, pop culture, and so on—you, the parents, will have by far the largest slice. Then, if you look at the actual makeup of your "slice," you might find factors such as time spent, conversation, example-setting, and family devotionals. Of all these, the greatest portion of your influence is the way you manage your anger.

Can you comprehend the critical nature of our subject? Of all the influences upon your children, you are the greatest. Of all the factors defining your influence, anger is the key. This is why we say handling anger in your home is the making or breaking of your children. Whether we like it or not, we set an example for them to follow, then we also influence them in several critical ways.

Inappropriate control of anger hurts children's self-esteem, sense of identity, ability to relate to others, perceptions of the world, stress management, and overall ability to function in society. Also, mismanagement of anger causes children to develop passive-aggressive, antiauthority, self-defeating attitudes. If not corrected by their late teen years, those attitudes will become deep-seated factors in basic character. Their own children will, in turn, be influenced by those attitudes. This is why the Old Testament often speaks of "the sins of the fathers" reverberating down through seven generations or more. It is crucial that we live and express our emotions wisely, not only because of how it affects us, but because of how it affects this world and the one that lies in the balance for tomorrow.

If parents handle their own anger maturely, they give children one of life's most powerful and fulfilling gifts. They build in children a potent life force that will assure that they grow to their own maturity without the afflictions that trouble so many adults. Every parent I know cares deeply about the emotional development and maturity of his or her children. They long to know that, when the time comes for them to leave this life, they will be succeeded by warm, caring, conscientious, successful, and well-loved sons and daughters.

But when anger rages out of control in a family, that goal simply isn't possible. Children are incredibly sensitive to the emotions of their parents. They cannot live in the same household without bearing the imprint of that anger. A single incident of mismanaged anger will cause severe and unforgettable pain, and a pattern of it will do permanent damage. On the other hand, mature handling of anger is a powerful force that will intensify the love between parent and child.

Think of each day as a short journey marked by several crossroads. We come to these forks in the road and decide our route—that is, how we will handle an issue emotionally. If we take the path of maturity, our children will walk proudly with us on a journey of growth and blessing. They will learn how to choose rightly. If we take the "low road," however, our children will come to feel that this is their destiny, their only choice—for certainly, if Mom or Dad could not walk a happier and less painful road, there must not be one to walk. If children never see what lies down the path of maturity, how can they know what wisdom and peace they would find there?

Some adults (men, in particular) don't make the wisest travelers in a strange city simply because they don't like stopping to ask directions. They take a wrong turn, then they complicate the problem by stubbornly insisting they can find their own way. Where our sons and daughters are concerned, we can't travel in that way. We have to manage anger in the wisest way possible, because of the situation itself and because of the example.

As the Greeks said, Know thyself. This chapter is written to help you understand how you handle anger, and to begin making whatever adjustments you need to make in your cycles of coping with it. I strongly recommend that you read this chapter, as well as the following one, before you go to sleep at night. Let your mind sort through the issues as you slumber. Review the chapters in depth so that the information is in the forefront of your mind. You'll find it easier to pledge yourself to handling your anger effectively and wisely during the crossroads of your next daily journey.

Just one day at a time—you are responsible for no more than that. Each day you make the right decisions and handle your anger properly, you're taking a positive step not just for today but for tomorrow. You're investing in your own future satisfaction, as well as the future well being of your children. Mishandled anger becomes a destructive cycle that finally does terrible damage in every direction. But well-handled anger, too, becomes habitual. And it bears positive fruit.

Twenty Questions

Most people have played the parlor game known as Twenty Questions. The game uses simple yes or no questions to unravel the identity of a mystery guest. You'll find a more serious group of 20 questions below. Most of these require a yes or no response, though you will find them anything but simple to consider. I strongly recommend that you take the time to work through this exercise.

As you confront each question, be brutally honest with yourself. Find the areas where you know you could and should do a better job. For instance, you may take responsibility for your behavior most of the time, but in certain circumstances you tend to fail to measure up to the standard you know you should be setting.

On those particular answers, you will want to do a bit more thinking.

1. Do you take responsibility for your behavior?
2. Do you keep your promises?
3. Do you feel generally positive or negative about your character and level of maturity?
4. Are you usually optimistic or pessimistic?
5. Are you still struggling with attitudes and events from your childhood and teenage years?
6. Do you often feel anger you cannot resolve?
7. Do you like who you have become? Do you have a plan for continued growth?
8. Does the idea of getting to know yourself better sound like a good adventure or a dangerous threat?
9. Do you show respect and fairness to each member of your family?
10. Do you show respect and fairness to those whom you manage at work? At church or in the community?
11. Do you often complain about those to whom you are subordinate at work? In the church or community?
12. Do you give an honest day's work for your pay?
13. Do you frequently complain about your spouse?
14. Do you recognize and cultivate the presence of God in your marriage and family life? In your personal life?
15. Do you have an ongoing plan for training your children in all areas of their lives, including the spiritual? Does this plan involve people in your extended family, church, and community?
16. Do you want your children to develop a character like yours?
17. When you face problems, do you generally ignore them, or do you think and pray about how you can confront and resolve them?

18. Are you open to new ideas and developments? Or do you find change threatening?
19. Are there people from whom you should ask forgiveness?
20. Are there matters for which you should make restitution?

Don't be alarmed to find yourself struggling with a few of these questions. I can't imagine anyone who would not. The important point is that you have a good idea of where you are in your journey and that you are willing to work on coming to a better place. Circle those questions that trouble you most, and spend some time writing out an action plan for how you can bring about positive change. Pray with dedication about those areas, and ask your spouse or close friends to pray with you.

Remember that God wants you to grow, and he doesn't desire that any of his children suffer. He wants the best for you and your children, and he stands ready to give you the power to live differently.

Taking Responsibility for Your Own Anger

In chapters 6 and 7, we talked about how not to manage anger. Now we need to talk about the right way to do things.

The first step is a willingness to take responsibility for anger. This is difficult because it is so easy to blame someone or something else. "I just can't help it," we say. "I wouldn't be angry if my boss didn't treat me this way. I wouldn't be angry if my children didn't pull these same stunts over and over again. I wouldn't be angry if my spouse hadn't said those things to me. I'll stop being angry when they stop treating me as they do."

We tell our children, "I don't like to shout at you in such a way that it frightens you, but I can't help it—you're the one who made me angry." Thus we blame our children for our anger. We use anger to justify our actions and attitudes, as if anger were a variable totally out of our control.

In fact, most people consciously or unconsciously seek out reasons to get angry so that they may then justify their own wrongdoing. Over the years, I have known of employees who have been fairly treated by their employers and yet have caused devastating harm to them. In each case, the employees used trivial and unrelated occurrences to justify their anger and then used that anger to justify their irresponsible behavior.

We have said that the first step is to take responsibility for anger. But even before that, we must identify the anger. That step can be more difficult than it might seem because there are many people who don't even realize when they're angry. Perhaps they feel jealous, frustrated, or hurt, and don't realize that the true root cause for that feeling is anger. It makes a great deal of difference to be able to say, "I know what this is: it's anger." Then, having put our finger on the real issue, we can consider what to do about it.

No one can take responsibility for your anger but you. To blame someone else is to hand them the keys to your psyche because you are giving them the power to upset you. Others are responsible for their actions, but only you are responsible for your reactions.

This distinction is a crucial one. Someone cuts in front of you in traffic, almost side-swiping your car. You are filled with rage. You want to do something to show that driver how you feel. You might take any action, from dangerous tailgating to immature gesturing and honking … to nothing at all. Why let that stranger in the red car determine your state of mind? Why give him that power? When you realize that it's normal to feel some anger but that you can choose not to react, you actually feel a great burden off your shoulders.

Blaming your child for your anger is inexcusable. It is also dangerous because you will bring in other unrelated anger issues. You became irritated today when you found out someone was gossiping about you at church, and you bring that anger to this situation. Your kids, who don't even know about the gossip, do something annoying and you unload on them. Unresolved anger is irrational; it won't distribute itself appropriately to the correct recipients. Innocent people get hurt. Then, after you have upset your children, you will be even angrier, even more frustrated, and you will take that into the church situation on Sunday. It's easy to see how the cycle perpetuates itself and how a spark somewhere can eventually lead to a forest fire.

Think about how you discharge your anger in relation to your children. The consequences can be tragic.

Dealing with Your Anger

Have you ever tried to discuss an unpleasant exchange, only to have the other person urgently plead with you to simply drop the subject? It's natural for us to want to put a nasty episode completely out of our minds. We're not proud of what we saw in ourselves in the heat of battle—best, it seems, not to think about it.

Unfortunately, we do need to think about it. We need to take a sober look at how we behaved, or we're likely to discharge our anger at the very next opportunity in the same way—or oversuppress it and start down that dangerous road of passive aggression. Many of us don't progress in the way we handle anger because we refuse to face an uncomfortable issue. But I recommend keeping a notebook of your progress in coping with anger. You'll be surprised by how much strength you'll derive from taking control of the situation through journaling it.

For example, you've had a bad experience at work. You received some treatment you don't feel you deserved, and you feel hurt (that is, angry). But you can't do or say anything about it on the job. What you can do is write out your feelings and keep writing until you come to a constructive idea for handling the situation and your feelings about it.

It is here that you're eager to ask what some of those constructive ideas might be. You can think of difficult situations in your own life, and you have no idea what to do with your anger, notebook or no notebook. Begin with the three points that combine to make the best way to handle anger. Handle it:

- Verbally
- Pleasantly
- Directly with the person with whom you are angry.

If at all possible, you want reconciliation and greater understanding between you.

If your problem is with a manager at work, and if it is appropriate to gently confront this person, you will want to do so in a calm and controlled manner. This means expressing your concern and then listening to the response. If the response is mature and you can negotiate a solution together, that's a true victory. You can feel good about how you handled a tough situation.

And here, of course, you're eager to make the point that things almost never work out that neatly. Your boss will react immaturely, and no solution will be forthcoming. Why, the situation might even be made worse!

Don't despair and don't ventilate. Seek out a friend, your spouse, or a counselor with whom you can share your feelings, not ventilate. Remember, ventilation stokes the fire of your anger with hot coals. Yet, if you keep it all inside, you will oversuppress it. Sharing your feelings with a trusted person will help.

Some people find relief in writing their feelings. I have counseled some folks to write a letter to the person with whom they are angry—then, in most cases, throw that letter away. Writing is a rational activity, and it often clarifies the truth for us. And when we write out our angry feelings, we see just how immature some of them are.

Reducing Your Susceptibility

I would now like to suggest some ways of reducing your proneness to anger—your susceptibility. You've noticed that some people are more anger-prone than others. You can do much to strengthen your natural defenses. The better your condition physically, spiritually, emotionally, the more effective you will be in handling anger.

You may not expect this subject to arise in a discussion of anger, but your body needs a healthy and balanced diet. You can get the specifics elsewhere, of course, but let me mention here that one little-known study has shown that too little fat in the diet can cause anxiety and irritability in some people. Your body needs an adequate amount of fat to remain healthy. I see increasing evidence of the wrong kind of dieting in my practice with behaviorally disturbed people. It is generally recommended that the fat in our diets should be 30 percent of total caloric intake.

This, of course, reminds us of the growing problem on the other end of the spectrum, in that many Americans are becoming increasingly overweight and out of shape.

Spiritual health is just as crucial for balance as good diet and physical fitness. I have discovered that far too often in my own experience. We all need to make regular times for prayer, confession, reading the Scriptures, fellowship with other Christians, and church attendance.

We should also think about the subject of depression, which can be a result of mismanaged anger. This is another disastrous cycle, because depressed people have increased problems in controlling their anger. Anger feeds depression, and depression in turn makes it more difficult for us to manage our anger.

This is a serious issue. Let me strongly counsel you to seek professional help if you feel that depression may play a part in your behavior. Keep in mind that children are acutely sensitive to depression in their parents. Also, parental depression can cause innumerable problems in the parent-child relationship, as well as in the child's development. Depressed behavior by the parent may cause guilt in the child. This makes it difficult for a parent to set and enforce limits.

When You Do Get Angry, Then What?

Let's say you've been having rocky times with a teenage daughter. Just being in the same room seems to threaten household peace. She breezes into the room and asks to go out with her friends on a school night, knowing that this request is clearly against the rules in your family. When you gently tell her so, she rolls her eyes, sighs heavily, and slams a door. This really gets your goat. What do you do? Stop and lecture? Ignore the whole thing?

Here's a key. If you can stay within the safe haven of three little words—firm but pleasant—then you'll handle the situation as well as it can be handled.

Remember, children are keenly aware of any anger or irritations you are feeling, and they are fearful that you will dump on them. When you are angry, they know it—and they feel profoundly relieved and grateful when you remain pleasant.

But you are human, and sometimes you won't be at your best. You may just unload your emotions on your child. What do you do then?

Personally, I use self-talk. When my children were young, I would tell myself something like, "You're losing it, Campbell. Don't make a fool of yourself and say something you will have to apologize for later." Other times, I told myself, "Cool it!" That usually worked. I might also say to myself, "If you don't want your children to be passive-aggressive and develop into irresponsible adults, you had better behave yourself."

I also made full use of an "escape hatch"—for me, the restroom. If self-talk didn't calm me down and I saw an angry confrontation in the works, I would say, "I've got to go to the restroom. I'll be back." And that's where I'd go—to rest my emotions. My children never followed me in, although some friends have told me that their young children have.

When I was alone, I thought about the situation—how and why I got so angry and how I could handle it to make it a positive learning experience for everyone, me included. Now, given a moment of solitude, I discovered many steps I could take to defuse the situation. I might think of a humorous incident from the past involving this particular child. Such a positive thought calmed me down, and it reinforced my pleasant feelings toward my child.

Let's face it: I was putting myself into an adult Time Out, just as we do for young children. Later, I conferred with my wife to get her perspective. This usually helped me to handle the next encounter better.

Even in the worst of circumstances, when you've lost your control and said or done something you regret, it's possible to bring something positive out of the negative. That begins with asking your child's forgiveness. This is a transcendent moment when your child receives a lesson in humility and forgiveness—forgiveness not only of you but of himself or herself as well. Your example of receiving forgiveness is very instructive for your son or daughter. We live in a world of miserable people incapable of forgiving others or themselves; what a powerful and priceless gift you give your children when you teach them mercy and grace.

A wise professor once taught me this lesson: "True intimacy comes from resolved conflict." I've come to believe those words with all my heart. In marriage, we draw closer than ever when we work through a problem together in the right way. But it's true in parent-child relationships as well. When you've had a terrible experience and you're not feeling very good about your child or yourself, keep this in mind: You actually have an opportunity to grow closer, though it may not seem so at all.

I always approach conflicts as opportunities for greater intimacy. But in order to resolve a conflict, I must first be able to handle my anger. If I can express it verbally and pleasantly and resolve the conflict, I will see my relationships grow and flourish.

When Mother's the Target

Let's assume you've done your best to provide a loving and relaxed home atmosphere for your growing children. You and your spouse are growing in your marriage relationship and moving toward greater levels of acceptance, forgiveness, and mutual support.

Even in such a home—perhaps especially in such a home—the mother may be the target of a child's anger. Children will often focus their rage at one particular parent, and that parent is likely to be the mother. The mothers, in turn, are distressed and confused. They feel that their children love them less than they love their father, or that they, the mothers, must not be very good at parenting. They often suffer from guilt and depression as a result.

That's unfortunate, because in most homes, all of this simply indicates that the mother is doing her job beautifully.

Why? Because most mothers have enjoyed, from the beginning, very special relationships with their children. The child feels so loved and secure with her that it's safe to express negative feelings. Children may be more unsure about how their father would react, but Mother will always be Mother. They know deep inside, from the time they were infants, that Mother is the one person in the world least likely to reject them. And now, though their angry attacks are hurtful, they're actually evidence of confidence in the relationship.

Of course, this doesn't mean that the mother should permit inappropriate expressions of anger. All of our rules from previous chapters still apply. But it's helpful to mothers to understand why they're the focus of the child's anger. It's also helpful to realize that the child's confidence sets the stage for training. As long as the child is bringing anger to the mother verbally, she and the father are in the position for training the child to handle anger correctly.

Imagine the reverse scenario: a household in which the child is unable to express anger verbally to parents. There would be no occasion for training, no "teachable moment." Nothing good could come of the child's anger. But it must come out somewhere. We want it to come out verbally, and when it does, there's a strong likelihood that the mother will be the recipient. She just needs to remember this doesn't mean she's a lesser parent or that she has done anything wrong.

What about single-parent homes? If the mother is the custodial parent, she will receive an even larger portion of the anger. The above reasons apply, but in this case the mother and child are together more often. As a matter of fact, passive-aggressive behavior could rear its ugly head if the child has stored up angry emotions about a divorce.

That child will take it all out on the mother, or whichever parent he or she is around most often. Imagine a scenario where the father is the noncustodial parent. He spends less time with the child; he isn't involved in the harsh details of daily conflict and discipline. From the mother's perspective, he seems to come riding in on Friday evenings on his white horse, bearing gifts, and headed for the amusement park with the delighted child. He doesn't sit home when that child has the mumps. He doesn't clean the dirty underwear and help with the homework. But he comes off well with the child, and he is on the receiving end of much less anger. The frustrated mother may feel that her child loves his father best and behaves better on those weekends with Dad. It doesn't seem particularly fair. I have often seen this phenomenon used against the custodial parent in court.

In such situations, what can the custodial mother do? Above all, she needs to cling to the truths we have already discussed. She needs to maintain her courage and hope and to fend off those feelings of guilt and discouragement.

This mother should remember that, for now, she may seem to have an unfair disadvantage, but the advantage she does enjoy is very real, if invisible. If she will handle her own anger and her child's anger well, good things are going to happen within this relationship. She, the mother, will be the parent who will win the deepest respect and love from the child in the long run.

9

Basic Training

The Finnigan's family computer uses special software. This filtering program supposedly makes it possible for the children to browse the Internet safely, without suddenly being confronted by pornography or profanity.

The Finnigans have also installed a "V-Chip" on the family room television. The V-Chip reads information encoded in a program's FCC rating, then permits or blocks the show based upon criteria pre-set by the parents.

Mr. and Mrs. Finnigan are very protective of their two little girls, ages four and seven. The parents realize, as many of us do, that we live in a society that has "lost its moral compass," in the words of Jeb Stuart Magruder. He might have been speaking for the soul of his generation.

Despite all their preventive maintenance measures, the Finnigans are beginning to realize the hard truth. Even if they should choose home schooling as the educational strategy for their children; even if they are restrictive about where their children can go, what they can see or hear, whom they can befriend—even if the parents do all they can to guard the hearts and minds of their little ones—their best efforts simply won't be enough.

There is no hiding from our world and its pervasive influences. The Finnigans now realize they can't always be there for their children any more than a mother bird can always "be there" when her babies make their first flight out of the nest. At some point, parents have to let offspring spread their wings and fly solo. Sooner or later, children must make their own decisions about the kinds of lives they will lead. And at that point, all the software and V-Chips in the world will be of little consequence.

That's why we have to do more than filter, censor, and avert our children's eyes. We need to train them to think, clearly and wisely. As columnist Ellen Goldman writes, "At some point between Lamaze and the PTA, it becomes clear that one of your main jobs as a parent is to counter the culture."[1] Whether or not it takes a village to raise a child, we cannot afford to leave the job to strangers. It's time to be "hands on" in the training areas that endure, and to take back the shaping and molding of the next generation.

By the time they reach adolescence, children need discerning minds. They need to evaluate for themselves what is right and wrong, who would make a good friend, and how their time should be spent. We need to realize that neither we nor the church will be training them in a vacuum. Many forces—Madison Avenue, Hollywood, academia, social pressure—will, at times, compete for the souls of our children.

Many parents simply don't realize this is going on in their children's lives. They simply don't comprehend the inflow of cultural influences that surround their kids. Then one day they are startled to see, living in their homes, teenage strangers who have slowly but effectively absorbed philosophies and lifestyle decisions from directions Mom and Dad never suspected. Drugs and drinking have gotten through the front door somehow. Premarital sex has found its way into the home. Radical ideas come from the lips of the kids who so recently nestled in their parents' laps as they read *Green Eggs and Ham*. This abrupt realization comes as a powerful blow to parents who have dedicated themselves to raising upright, successful children.

My shoulders have felt the tears of many bewildered parents, wondering where they went wrong. I sit with them and talk over the history of their households, asking a few probing questions. In cases where children have chosen rebellious directions, we've usually found some combination of two factors—passive-aggressive anger and a lack of parental training.

But the first all-important foundations are laid as we train children to think clearly. Some parents assume their children will do so on their own simply because they have good minds and are busy collecting information in school. Knowledge and wisdom, as we all know, are two entirely separate categories. Parents need to intentionally teach their children how to think in correct and rational ways, even as they train them in the discipline of handling anger.

Let's look at some good opportunities for basic training.

Reading Together

We all enjoy the intimate moments of sharing a good book before bedtime. It's comforting to know that such an activity is just as valuable as it is pleasant. Take every opportunity to read together, beginning when children are infants.

You enjoy the quietness and warmth of your child during these moments; your child enjoys the touch, the attention, the soft tones of your voice. It's no wonder that strong bonding results from reading together, and that's why you'll want to choose your literature carefully. For little ones, look for stories of comfort and security. As they grow older, find narratives that promote strong values. Happily, publishers offer excellent, colorful Bible storybooks for every age level.

You can find parental guides on the Internet and in other places; allow me to offer you a few recommendations. Gladys Hunt's *Honey for a Child's Heart* provides a guide to children's classics. To help parents distinguish between a good book and one lacking significant value, she writes, "A good book has a profound kind of morality—not a cheap, sentimental sort which thrives on shallow plots and superficial heroes, but the sort of force which inspires the reader's inner life and draws out all that is noble."[2]

I also recommend *Books That Build Character* by William Kilpatrick and Gregory and Suzanne M. Wolfe because the authors provide an extensive list of books and stories. They also offer us guidance in using literature to teach moral values.[3]

You may already be familiar with William Bennett's *The Book of Virtues*. This collection of stories, poems, and fables is chosen for enjoyable family reading and as a basis for discussions about values and morality.[4]

Tune in to your child's wavelength as you read together. How is she responding to the story and the message? Pause occasionally to draw attention to a valuable point, to measure attention, or to simply enjoy a laugh together. Find opportunities to ask what your child is thinking. This will enable you to enter the discussion on your child's interest level. For example, you might be sharing a story about a little boy lost in the woods. As your child expresses concern for the character, you'll have the opportunity to acknowledge and affirm your child's kind, caring nature. As simple as it sounds, you'll be accentuating positive values and virtues.

What is happening as you read together? Your child is learning to think and to analyze a situation, to make appropriate value judgments in an objective way. Who is behaving in the right way in the story? Who is doing wrong? Why?

As you discuss these issues from the distance of a storybook, you will be rehearsing the same kinds of judgments to be made about real situations. For example, all children blame inappropriately: "It's his fault! He started it!" Anger brings about irrational thinking; it helps to spend time learning to take the data and judge it objectively. Fantasy is the opportunity to rehearse real life. The rocking chair and the warmth are your allies in creating an ideal classroom situation.

Another wonderful benefit of reading is its ability to offer new perspectives—for adults as well as children. A young child has had limited experience in the world. Books can open up whole new vistas, new situations, and new possibilities. Read sympathetically about the lepers brought to Jesus and you can teach empathy and sympathy—two qualities all too rare today. The healthy emotional development of your child requires both.

Sympathy is understanding the feelings of another; empathy is entering into another person's point of view. Sympathy is understanding the journey someone has made; empathy is actually walking an emotional mile in their shoes. If your son is aware of the difficult home situation of a misbehaving classmate, his sympathy makes him capable of being more tolerant of the irritating behavior. If you have an in-depth discussion with him about that situation and the daily difficulties the other child must face, your son may develop real empathy—an excellent indicator that your child will grow up to be a compassionate, caring adult.

I remember the pride I felt in my six-year-old granddaughter, Cami. One of her classmates was disliked and rejected by the other children. But Cami understood this girl's pain and made a special effort to reach out as a friend. I have every confidence she will be the type of person who will make a positive difference in our world as she comes of age.

That's all we can ask, isn't it? We want our children to be compassionate and caring. You are your child's guide in the realm of emotions. As you travel together through the colorful and stimulating worlds of children's literature, you'll encounter stories about love, anger, kindness, sadness, guilt, pity, and more. You can identify and talk about these as if pointing out beautiful flowers in a garden. Your children will build an "emotional repertoire" that will serve them well as they grow.

And don't forget two other kinds of stories: tales from your childhood and tales from your imagination. Your memories help children see that you, too, have lived through the same adventures of growing up. Stories spun from your imagination will surprise and delight them and possibly stimulate their own creativity. You might even exercise their imaginative gifts by letting them help create the scene, the characters, and the plot.

Talking Together

Communication is paramount in any relationship and absolutely essential to personal growth. You'll never know what issues your child is facing unless you're constantly in touch with his or her feelings through conversation. Certainly, that moment of key information may come while you're reading together, but it's just as likely to come at the dinner table, in the car, or at bedtime. Expect the unexpected.

As you talk things over, you hope to discover how your child responds to problems. As you assess where your children are, you will be able to help them face the real world of their age level. You want to teach children to respond to difficulties in optimistic ways and help them to become hopeful persons.

People with tendencies toward pessimism respond internally in ways that are totally different from more optimistic people. Excellent research by Martin Seligman and others has shown three important differences between the two types.

Pessimists tend to consider a problem or mishap as permanent, as though the effects will last forever. Second, pessimists see a problem as pervasive, as though it will ruin their entire lives. And third, they tend to blame themselves for the problem, thus causing guilt and depression.

Optimists are quite the opposite. Seeing mishaps as temporary, they're capable of putting these incidents aside and moving on. Second, they see problems as localized, affecting only a part of their lives. Because they don't dwell on the problems, they can keep their minds grounded in the realm of the positive. Third, optimists tend to blame others for their problems.[5]

Of course, neither response is always the correct one, and we can't use this research as a fail-safe guide. But I have found it helpful in keeping my own thinking and emotional responses on track, as well as in teaching children.

Imagine that your daughter goes out for the soccer team but doesn't make the cut. She comes home in a terrible mood, sulking and behaving irritably. Your first reaction is to tell her to "chin up and show her bright smile," but you know that's not the right course of action. You want her to express her anger verbally, right? Yes, and you can expect it to be unpleasant. Just remind yourself that putting up with her anger may not be a picnic for now, but this is the very best time and place for her to deal with her feelings.

If you handle your daughter well when she expresses anger, she will be drawn to your example for coping with disappointment and frustration. If she is young enough to enjoy reading stories together, you could find one in which a main character suffers disappointment. The story would provide comfort ("See, it happens to all of us.") and guidance in approaching similar problems. After the story, you might invite her to verbalize her discouragement and some possible approaches to the way she is feeling. What a priceless opportunity to guide your daughter to become a hopeful individual. What an occasion for showing how Christianity provides guidance and answers.

As children grow older, of course, you'll want to talk more about specific feelings involved in their responses. Now when your daughter comes home sulking, you could discuss hurt, pain, disappointment, anger, discouragement, hate, or any other feeling she is experiencing. It's so important to help her verbalize her feelings so she won't act them out behaviorally. After you've gotten her into the habit of verbalizing, the next step will be to move her from unpleasant expression toward a pleasant one. When the time comes that she can deal with her anger verbally and inoffensively, you've reached a crucial milestone that will benefit her—and everyone in her world—for a lifetime.

You will also want to use such situations to help your child handle blame. It's vital for children to learn whether blame is appropriate and where it should be directed. Far too much blaming is destructive in nature. In our example of not making the soccer team, your daughter needs to learn that blame would be inappropriate; after all, not everyone is fortunate enough to make the final squad. This time she didn't make the cut, but in other areas, she will excel. She needs to realize that today's disappointment is no one's fault. Tell her that trying out for a team takes courage; you're proud of her efforts for giving her best and taking the risk of rejection—that requires a strong person.

Are these words likely to bring a big smile and turn her mood around? Not particularly. Your daughter is still likely to be upset. But you can be certain that the lesson has been received. Much of learning is invisible. Only later do we realize we've been successful as teachers. If you've talked compassionately with your child, helped her verbalize her feelings, and provided comfort and encouragement, you've accomplished a great deal. She will feel loved beneath her tears; she will remember; she will feel gratitude in the years to come.

Being Available

As you well know, parenting is far from finished as children reach the teenage years; stormy times lie ahead. Your children may seem less attentive to your advice and guidance, but they need it profoundly.

Your greatest goal is to make yourself available to your children and also to structure times when the normal adolescent defenses are down. When might that be? Look for occasions when both parent and teenager are relaxed and unpressured; instances when neither parent nor child feels the need to say or do anything. These opportunities sneak up on us in the little moments: waiting in line at the drive-through window; walking to the mall from the parking lot; the five-minute sequence of television commercials. Teenagers are more likely to be relaxed and to be themselves. It's a good time for clear communication.

You'll need to be patient to wait for the best moment for the best results. You'll also need to remind yourself that teenagers are not miniature adults. They are children in transition who have the same basic needs as younger children do. Foremost of these, of course, is unconditional love. But they also need help in identifying and understanding their feelings.

This is not as easy as it may seem at first. Children often show the symptoms of anger when the feeling is actually one of rejection, stress, loneliness, inadequacy, or weakness. You might want to ask, "What are you so angry about?" But your child will not be able to answer, because the problem is not anger but something else. You're in danger of greeting the wrong emotion with the wrong response, so it's very important that you and your child learn to identify exactly what the problem really is. Then the child can express what he's feeling, and you can respond appropriately.

Another approach for these random moments is one I call predicting. You have some experience with life, and you can look ahead toward the likely issues of your child's life. This makes it possible to prepare your child for the challenges he or she will face. School children, for example, need to feel comfortable and accepted within their peer groups. This makes them extremely sensitive to rejection, criticism, and teasing. Thinking ahead in your child's life, you can help him or her think about the issue before it rears its ugly head. You can ask what your child will do when a bully appears, when he or she feels left out, and even how to help to make other children feel better accepted.

There are several ways to do this, but storytelling is my favorite. I tell a tale in which a child is poorly treated by his friends, then learns how to make the very best of the situation. I never build fear or dread, of course; it's important to emphasize the positive because we want children to look forward to social interchanges.

You can also tell some true stories—the ones you have lived through. You may not have encountered the exact same challenges as those of your child, but you struggled with your own feelings of hurt and frustration. The feelings are the key; they resonate in others when we share them. Your child will be encouraged to know that you've been there, done that, and lived to tell the tale.

No matter what occurs in the lives of your children, you want them to behave as people of integrity who tell the truth, keep their promises, and assume responsibility for their own behavior. Such virtues don't "grow wild"; they need to be planted, nurtured, and harvested in the lives of our children. Reading together, sharing old family stories, and talking through present-day scenarios will all do their part in building the right character in children.

Meanwhile, as you try to nurture integrity, your children will be facing the constant temptation to behave in other ways. Their friends will contribute to that as will television and the culture of moral expediency that surrounds us. We could worry about that, but we know that we have our children's ears. We have the "inside track" in the shaping of our young people, and there is no TV show, video game, or school friend who will have a greater influence than we as parents will. Those little moments here and there will add up. In the course of a child's development, they will finally derive the sum of all your efforts to develop a strong and responsible human being.

Handling Misbehavior

No matter what you do, how many books you read, or how well you prepare yourself, bad behavior will be an issue if you are a parent. What are its various forms? How will you face them? Here are a few common ones.

Whining. Whining is irritating! You may need to fight the urge to dump your anger on the child: "Stop that whining right now or you will be punished!"

If you do this, you have lost the battle. When you dump anger on your child, you are providing more ammunition to use against you. You're also letting the child know that he or she really upsets you. Later, when the child wants to push your emotional buttons, he will know that whining is an effective strategy for manipulating you. The more anger you show, the more whining you can expect—not to mention that you are working toward forcing your child to oversuppress anger and develop antiauthority and passive-aggressive attitudes and behaviors.

Make no mistake—your anger toward whining is counterproductive.

Some parents respond to their child's whining by fighting fire with fire—whining right back. "Here is what you sound like," the parent is saying. The child experiences parental whining as hostility, and this is a poor model for managing anger. A child also has the separate frustration of being ridiculed and mimicked. Whining back is another poor choice.

How can you respond positively to this problem? We've all heard the whispered advice: "Just ignore him!" This is easier said than done at times, but for most children it does work. Your behavior can't be manipulated when you refuse to respond. If the whining continues, however, you can calmly and coolly say, "I can't hear you when you talk in that voice. Use your nice voice so I can understand what you want."

Sometimes that approach is a winner—but not always. If the whining doesn't let up, your first priority is to be certain you're still calm. Don't give in to anger because then the whining has won and you (and your training) have lost. Then, when you're doubly sure you're still calm, use sheer fun as a distraction. This is a favorite approach of mine. Depending on the age of your child, place a tempting idea for fun in front of him or her.

Some whiners can be stubborn. If the behavior continues despite all your patience and strategy, then leave the child alone in a safe place with the assurance that you'll be happy to discuss anything your child wants as soon as he's found his "nice voice."

Whining is one of those problems with no easy cure. If you have a born whiner in the family, you'll have to use all the strategies outlined above—and plenty of patience. Still you'll find yourself coping with the problem. You can cut down on some of the whining, but don't expect the problem to go away overnight.

In extreme situations, you can always use a Time Out or positive reinforcement. We'll explore these options later.

Tantrums and Violent Outbursts. Preschool children are especially prone to using temper tantrums as a way of controlling their parents. What triggers them? Tiredness, thirst, hunger, heat, cold, or pain can spark fresh outbursts. Smaller children lack the level of self-control adults might call upon to calm their emotions. Children need parents to help them learn to control their behavior.

Temper tantrums can be an even greater challenge for parents than whining, especially in public settings. But many of the same guidelines and strategies apply. Parents need to control their own anger and, no matter how hard it may be for us, simply ignore the tantrum. I would suggest getting busy with a household chore—preferably one that makes a bit of noise.

Again, a child performing to no audience will often give up the act. But if the tantrum continues, you might give your child a time limit for regaining control. At the end of that time, you might reward the misbehavior with a Time Out, loss of privileges, or extra chores. But your calmness is the key. It communicates to your child that you have firm control and will not be manipulated by tantrums. Remaining calm takes tremendous self-discipline. Try humming, singing softly, or visualizing pleasant memories or future plans. Singing or humming, as a matter of fact, can help soothe the child.

As children reach school age, their anger is likely to be triggered by social factors—rejection by peers, criticism, judgments that seem unfair, or perhaps a perception of insecurity in parental love.

It helps to know the basic methods of calming down in the midst of turmoil. For parents and children alike, deep muscle relaxation is very helpful. Choose a happy and relaxed moment for teaching this technique so issues of present anger won't get in the way. Teach your child to tense, then relax, each body part—left foot, left leg, right foot, right leg, etc. It's extra effective to suggest that your child imagine a favorite cartoon or fantasy character sharing the exercise with your child.

As my children grew older, I selected a certain sign or word to link to relaxation. I could then use that sign or word as a signal when I saw that they were becoming upset. This often helped them cool down an emotional buildup. The sign I used was to place my right index finger next to my nose and then suddenly move it forward. The signal I used was, "Cool it," said in a soft tone. Incidentally, if I started to get upset or tense, I would tell myself, "I think I had better cool it."

Communicating Clearly

Thomas Gordon, author of *Parent Effectiveness Training*, has long advocated the use of "I" messages rather than "you" messages. As parents use "I" messages, they train their children to express feelings (including anger) without developing the destructive habit of blaming.[6]

For example, a teenager is preoccupied with thoughts of a used car he wants to buy or some crisis involving his friends. The mandate to leave his muddy boots outside has slipped his mind completely. He tracks mud and slime across the freshly waxed kitchen floor and onto the living room carpet. Mom is likely to look up and say, "Now look what you've done!" That statement, of course, is certain to provoke anger and tension. Instead, Mom might say, "I feel upset when mud is brought into the house."

At first glance, you might have trouble visualizing yourself making such an I-statement. But offered in a calm tone, and given its avoidance of blaming, the statement creates less tension. It's an effective "transition sentence" to a cool, calm discussion about avoiding muddy tracking the next time. The real payoff comes when the teenager begins to make I-statements of his own, because he will be a step closer to taking responsibility for his actions.

Is silence a form of communication? It certainly can be, and it has a number of forms of its own within the household. One important use of silence is the cool-down period after an episode of anger or tension. Meg Eastman comments that when the emotional current is still running high in parent or child, an attempt at discussion can actually be a bad idea. It simply intensifies the frustration on both ends. Silence helps restore the peace, inside and outside.

Ms. Eastman also points out another value of silence—at times when children want to take up the subject of nonnegotiable rules. It's less than helpful to discuss what has already been settled because it encourages a fresh buildup of anger and frustration. On those occasions, the hardest task for most parents is to just be quiet.[7]

Setting Limits

Behavioral problems seldom have quick or tidy solutions. Every home reaches a point when there must be penalties of some kind—perhaps loss of privileges or some other punishment. When a child is out of control, being defiant, or challenging parental authority, we need to thoughtfully select an appropriate response.

Parents have five ways to control a child. Two are positive, two are negative, and one is neutral. They are:

Positive: Requests; gentle physical manipulation.
Negative: Commands; punishment.
Neutral: Behavior Modification.

The effectiveness of any of these is going to depend on whether and how much we are keeping our children's emotional tanks full.

Requests are a very good option. They're positive, and they can calm anger. A request might be, "Would you do this for me?" "Would you try to speak in a pleasant tone of voice?" Strong, positive, nonverbal messages are delivered, such as, "I respect you as a person. I also respect the fact that you have feelings and opinions. I expect you to take responsibility for your behavior."

It would be a wonderful world if requests always worked, but you probably already realize that they don't. Sometimes we must use commands. Because a command is an imperative statement and carries a negative connotation, it may elicit anger. It seems to convey, "I'm not concerned about your feelings or opinions right now. I'm not concerned about your taking responsibility for your own behavior. The issue is for you to do what I say." As a matter of fact, we are also sending this message: "I am taking responsibility for your behavior."

Gentle physical manipulation is a positive way to control a child's behavior. This works especially well with young children, as when you lead a toddler away from a hot stove or toward a kind of play that will be more acceptable.

Punishment is the second negative form of behavior control. Parents tend to assume that punishment should be used whenever they see misbehavior. This mistake is what I call the "punishment trap." Parents who rely strongly on punishment will provoke a great deal of needless anger in their children. They will also force the child to oversuppress anger and develop passive-aggressive attitudes and behavior. This is especially dangerous if the parents are angry when they use punishment.

Yes, we must occasionally use punishment, but we need to use it wisely and carefully. And we can avoid many problems associated with punishment by planning ahead. I recommend sitting down with your spouse or a good friend and planning the appropriate punishment for an offense. As we all know, children are deeply concerned about the idea of "being fair." The punishment must fit the crime. A child knows when a parent is being too harsh or too lenient. When the time comes for punishment, it's important to have already chosen your means of punishment. Advance planning helps you guard against letting your anger influence your behavior, and your child will be grateful.

Time Out

Most parents are familiar with the strategy of a Time Out. A child is asked to stand or sit in a specified place for a certain length of time. This procedure can be quite effective when a child's anger is out of control. The widely accepted length of time is one minute for every year of a child's age.

Therefore, if your six year old is calm after six minutes of Time Out, by all means praise her behavior. If she remains out of control, tell her that Time Out will be over as soon as she has regained her self-control. If your child is destructive to toys or property, find a place you know is childproof, with only a few of the child's toys or books. Time Outs are usually the first punishment for dealing with anger or rage.

Loss of Privilege and Restrictions

What if Time Out doesn't work? Think about your child's favorite TV program, toy, or activity. Loss of privilege can make a strong point. There are many children who simply cannot tolerate missing a certain cartoon or being deprived of a toy. When they realize that restrictions loom before them as a possibility, they will be motivated to control their behavior.

Restrictions are more appropriate to older children and teenagers. But used too often, they can backfire. You may forget what has been restricted, or you may discover that the details are unenforceable. If so, you've undermined your control of the household and decreased your children's respect for you.

Use restrictions wisely and after a good deal of thought, making sure the situation is important enough to justify the penalty. They can be very effective when they're applied properly.

Compensation and Chores

What if "innocent bystanders" come into the equation? Your teenage daughter has not only dented the fender of the family car, but she knocked down the neighbor's mailbox. Or perhaps your ten-year-old son broke the neighbor's window with a baseball.

In such cases, you will want your child to make compensation or restitution. This should, of course, be appropriate to the child's age and ability to repay or make a sacrifice. An apology is always in order. But compensation may be more complex than the price of a new window or a new mailbox. You may need to consult others to determine a fair amount.

Doing extra chores can be an effective means of reinforcing the consequences of misbehavior. If you use this method, be sure the time and number and difficulty of chores are appropriate to the child and also to the offense.

Behavior Modification

Behavior modification is a psychological trend that refers to a system that uses:

- Positive reinforcement: adding something positive into a child's environment;
- Negative reinforcement: withdrawing something positive from a child's environment;
- Punishment: adding something negative into a child's environment.

Behavior modification has its place in child rearing. However, it is a mistake to use it as the main basis for relating to a child.

An example of positive reinforcement is to reward a child's good behavior by giving a treat. A negative reinforcement might be to withhold a television program for inappropriate behavior. An example of punishment, sometimes called aversion technique, is to pinch the child on the trapezius for inappropriate behavior.

It is my definite view that problems arise when parents substitute "behavior mod" for emotional nurture. What children need is love, and enough of it to fill their emotional tanks. Behavior modification techniques tend to be cold, clinical efforts to program a child rather than train and guide. Children definitely feel the difference, and they feel unloved.

There is also the problem of the value system you create through behavior modification. The child will be motivated by reward rather than rightness. In the end, his attitude will be, "What's in it for me?"

Wise parents use behavior modification sparingly. Some of the discipline techniques already discussed, such as Time Outs, fall into this category. Behavior modification tends to be formal and impersonal and should generally be used for specific, recurring behavioral problems for which the child is neither sorry nor defiant.

One good example is the common problem of quarreling siblings. Our boys fought frequently when they were five and nine. We could ask them to stop, but before long they were bickering again. Punishments were only partially successful, and they were unpleasant for everyone. Finally, we tried a reward system. We took a piece of poster board and made a chart for the family to see. There were stars—one star for every minute of peace, gradually increasing the time intervals until the fighting stopped. We gave each boy an appropriate reward for a certain number of stars.

A word of warning about this technique—it takes time, consistency, real effort, and patience. Don't start it unless you are prepared to stay with it. Otherwise, it will fail.

One final word: In every part of your family relationships, emphasize the positive whenever you can. You'll be more effective when discipline is necessary, as well as in the total training of your children.

Be alert for opportunities to provide positive reinforcement— not just for an "all-A" report card or a clean room, but in the "little" times. The most powerful gestures of love and encouragement you'll ever offer are the everyday, natural, nonverbal ways you give approval: listening attentively to your child, smiling and laughing together, spontaneous hugs, time spent together.

Those natural motivators have nothing to do with the behavior modification model. But they have everything to do with forming unbreakable bonds of love and commitment between parents and children.

10

75/25: How Children Face Authority

Three decades is a considerable period of time for working in one focused area. I've spent over 30 years observing the ways people behave, particularly in families. Naturally, I've come to a number of conclusions of various kinds. One of these has to do with the ways we tend to respond to authority.

Most people are either pro-authority or antiauthority. That should come as no news to anyone. But I've also observed that about one individual in four belongs to the pro-authority group, while the other three are antiauthority. In different time periods and in different cultures, perhaps the figures might be different. But in our contemporary social context, I'm convinced that we're made up of "25-percenters" (pro) and "75-percenters" (anti).

Within those groups, of course, there are variations in the degree to which any individual holds that stance. But if you selected four people at random off a busy street, you would generally find that one of them would tend to be naturally submissive to authority, while three of them might tend to oppose it. If you took your sampling in a church, the percentage of 25-percenters would actually be much higher than 25 (this has been my observation). Then again, if you took your sampling at a political demonstration, a good deal more than 75 percent of the participants might be 75-percenters.

Are you confused? We're simply saying that these figures are generally true, but they vary according to the kind of group we're talking about.

Perhaps it's helpful to use a visual aid. The graph entitled "Attitudes Toward Authority," shown at the end of this chapter, depicts the two groups as well as the variations in intensity within their groups. The bell-shaped curves show that a 25-percenter can be mild, moderate, or extreme, just as a 75-percenter can be anywhere from mildly antiauthority to extremely antiauthority.

I imagine you don't remember selecting one of these groups, nor can you recall attending a meeting of either tribe. The truth is that, in general, the groups choose us; that is, we tend to be born with our basic attitudes toward authority as surely as we're born with blue eyes or a gift for music. This attitude toward authority can vary to some extent based upon upbringing and environment, but the basic trait remains dominant.

You might be tempted to connect these groups to the popular understandings of personality types—introvert vs. extrovert, for example. But the truth is that an extrovert may be either pro- or antiauthority; it's the same with an introvert. In both groups, we find all kinds of people. It's the same with the traditional DISC model of personality traits (sanguine, choleric, and so on). There's simply no correlation between personality types and authority attitudes.

Authority is a significant issue in any life. How we respond to nearly anything that comes along will touch on the way we handle authority, which, in turn, is very much dependent upon inborn tendencies. All the more reason we need to understand this provocative side of ourselves and our children.

We like to think of our lives as a series of choices, a journey over which we have supreme control. Yet we need to realize that our parents genetically handed down to us our basic temperaments, tendencies, gifts, and traits—such a great portion of the basic machinery of our personalities. To a large extent, then, your personality is the hand you were dealt at birth, but it's not a question of "better" or "worse" personalities. It's a question of difference. There is still a great deal of freedom in how we use that basic machinery. We want to understand, as clearly as possible, the basic natures of our children; then we want to work to enhance and enrich those natures that they might be turned to good in the world.

Twenty-five-Percenters

Twenty-five-percenters are born with a need to live and serve under authority. Their quest in life is for approval and praise. They are happiest when someone tells them what to do and how to divide their time.

You might immediately think, "That's the kind of child I want! Give me unquestioning obedience in a child." This would seem to make parenting very simple. But of course that's not how life works. Twenty-five-percenters are just as difficult to raise as 75-percenters. They need much more guidance in how to think for themselves, how to stand on their own two feet, and how to be less dependent. They are also easily controlled by guilt, since they are so prone to it. The rest of us, including their parents, tend to sense this and push those very buttons without even realizing it. Having exploited the guilt, the parents then pride themselves in having raised well-behaved, disciplined children.

Julie is the oldest of five children. She is a quiet and obedient girl whose parents, Evelyn and Richard, are subtly controlling her. One day, the girl asked her mother if she could attend a friend's swimming party. Her mother replied, "Oh, I'm sorry, Julie. I'd planned to meet your father for dinner downtown. I was hoping you could watch your brothers and sisters for me. Oh, well, never mind. I'll do it another time."

Julie instantly felt torn inside. She knew her mother, Evelyn, rarely got out of the house, but she deeply wanted to go to the swimming party. All her friends would be there, and she seldom asked her parents for anything. But then again, she thought of how awful she would feel if she realized her mother were giving up time away just so Julie could go to a party.

"Go ahead, Mom," Julie said after a short inner debate. "My swimsuit is faded anyway. I'd hate my friends to see me swimming in it. You go on and meet Daddy for dinner."

Over time, it had become easier for Evelyn to ask Julie to stay with the children because Julie never complained. In fact, Evelyn had come to believe that Julie actually enjoyed the task—as in fact she did, once in a while. But many were the times she'd rather have been doing other things, and deep inside she may have realized she was bearing too much burden. But guilt can be a very powerful motivator.

Twenty-five-percenters are easy to manage when they're young. Their parents are often overheard telling other parents, "If you would just be more firm with your child, she would be like Julie." It's always a mistake to use someone else's "template" in raising our children, of course. One may be very different than another. In the long run, children can be damaged by parents who impose inflexible systems.

When parents control their children with guilt, they are controlling them in the worst possible way. Twenty-five-percenters are so eager to please that they are easily crushed. They take everything personally and seriously. They also live in fear of hurting someone or doing something wrong. Because they tend to be perfectionists, they want to do everything exactly right. A little bit of criticism can smash their egos and make them feel so guilty that they fail to develop in their own individual directions.

It's difficult to blame parents who are blind to this reality. They enjoy having a nice, well-behaved child who always does exactly what he is told to do and never gives anyone a hard time. But Mom and Dad need to realize their children are harboring many private feelings. Fearing criticism, they're desperately afraid of sharing those feelings, which they may not even trust anyway, because such children are so critical of themselves. They only want approval and freedom from guilt, and they will bear many burdens—some lifelong, including the burden of inner regret—to keep that peace.

Twenty-five-percenters have such high expectations that each day can be a disappointment. Even if every event in a day is good but one, they will see only that one that could have gone better. Therefore, 25-percenters are prone to depression.

Brett is a sophomore in high school. He has just come home with an A on a math test, an A on an English quiz, and yet another A on a book report. What a great day! That afternoon, he hit a home run to drive in the winning run for his team.

Brett comes home smiling and whistling as he reads the note from his mom. She's going to be late, it seems. That's OK by Brett, who is on his way to the bowling alley anyway. He opens the closet and reaches for his red bowling shirt, but it's gone. He discovers it in the laundry basket, with dark stains on it.

Just like that, Brett's day is ruined. His team is bowling in a tournament and he has no shirt! The three As, the home run, and all the other good things about his current life are suddenly invisible to him. Another day falls short of perfection and is therefore a failure.

Brett's story illustrates the way a 25-percenter thinks. He can easily become depressed over some trifle. Depression, as we know, leads to anger. But Brett wants above all to please, so he bottles up that anger, causing the depression to become more powerful. This in turn causes more anger, which the child directs inward toward himself.

The 25-percenter can suffer from years of guilt manipulation, when his parents have no idea what is happening inside of him. He has not been taught to think for himself or to express his feelings verbally. As a consequence, he is on his way toward becoming a depressed and angry adult.

All humans need to feel loved and worthy; 25-percenters magnify these needs. But Mom and Dad don't realize the child's low self-esteem, so they can't fill the emotional tank, which runs on empty. All too often, the child seeks acceptance and self-worth outside the home. By the time the child is a teenager, he or she may be involved in destructive behavior.

Seventy-Five-Percenters

My wife is named Pat, and we have two sons. Dale is our 25-percenter who was born asking, "Dad, is there anything you and Mom would like me to do for you?"

David, on the other hand, arrived in the world with a brisk command that could be heard by everyone in shouting distance: "Would you people please step out of the way? I have a life to live, and I would like to get on with it with as little interference as possible!"

David was one of those "I'd rather do it myself" kids, and there was never any doubt about how he was feeling. These children want to do their own thinking and make their own decisions. They become angry when anyone tells them what to do. They're deeply driven to learn things on their own.

You might think 75-percenters would be much harder to raise, but you would be wrong. Even though they are born with an anti-authority attitude, they require the same amount of patience, love, and understanding as their more compliant siblings.

The drive to think for themselves gives the 75-percenters a natural talent for leadership. And I actually find it easier to keep this kind of child under control than to teach 25-percenters how to think for themselves. However, this child is likely to become angry when you are trying to train and discipline.

When our David was nearly 14, he announced one Sunday morning, "I'm not going to church today."

"Oh, come on, David," I replied, "you know that you have a good time once you're there."

He gave in and went with us and didn't say any more about it for a few weeks. And then, out of the blue, he announced, "I'm not going to church today. I told you before that I didn't want to go, and I'm not going."

This time I could see that it was useless to talk with him more—he was so determined that forcing him would have created an anti-church attitude that could have been difficult to reverse. I wanted to handle this without alienating David so that we could keep him on the road to maturity.

"Do you like Sunday school?" I asked.

"Yeah, I don't mind Sunday school."

"Well, then I'll tell you what we'll do. You go to Sunday school; then your mother or I will drive you home and stay here with you during church."

David agreed to this. Knowing that he was a 75-percenter, Pat and I wanted to prevent the anger toward spiritual things that can develop when these matters are forced. David was naturally anti-authority, so we chose for the moment not to pressure him. We didn't feel that we were being permissive; rather that we had a plan. David knew how we believed and was just testing us.

After this arrangement went on for four or five weeks, I could tell that it was getting old for David. He also realized that his mother and I were suffering because of it—we wanted to be in church together, of course. Finally, he said, "Oh, all right, I'll go to church for your sakes." And that was that.

I can't promise such a strategy will work for every 75-percenter. The key factor is the total relationship you have with your child. Above all, keep things positive and avoid authoritarian tactics, particularly in relationship to spiritual matters. We all know the swelling numbers of children who were raised in the church, only to leave when they were grown. We could speculate on the various reasons for this phenomenon, but we know that some of them are acting out their long-simmering resentment. You don't want your child to end up on that side of the fence.

In chapter 6, we talked about the one "normal" period of passive aggression in our children: the early teen stage. When you see it, don't panic or feel that you've failed as a parent. Just remember that passive-aggressive behavior goes for the jugular. It arises from anger and wants to strike out, so where are the likely targets? Church, as we've seen, could be one. Messy rooms may be a way of pushing Mom's buttons. And you can certainly expect passive-aggressive behavior to manifest itself in the area of schoolwork. Why? Anything particularly important in the home is a particularly likely target for this kind of behavior—and school performance matters greatly to nearly every parent.

When 75-percenters begin to do poorly in school, Mom and Dad need to resist the impulse to overreact. We've already discussed the fact that resistance only increases the passive-aggressive behavior. Appeals to reason never succeed because this behavior is not rational. The more you make of the situation, the worse things will become. Mothers and fathers want to stand right over their kids, arms crossed, and see that every assignment is done. But as long as parents and teachers get heavily involved and begin taking responsibility for the grades, why should the teenager? The result is that the child will become even more detached from responsibilities.

In chapter 6, I related how our older son, David—an extreme 75-percenter—allowed his grades to plummet in the eighth and ninth grades. I also explained how we handled that situation around our house and how our patience paid off in the long run. David learned a great lesson about life that he wouldn't have learned if we had stepped in and interfered. As it happened, he managed to arrest his plunging grade point average and get into the college of his choice.

Dale, our 25-percenter, never wavered in his approach to schoolwork. It pleased him to please his teachers and parents, and he continued to make excellent grades all through high school.

Thirteen- to fifteen-year-olds align themselves unconsciously (and sometimes consciously) against nearly everything. They frown about school. They roll their eyes about church. They sigh wearily about nearly any subject you might raise. This is especially true of the 75-percenters who are angry most of the time. Unpleasant as it may be, we need to keep the anger flowing from their mouths instead of finding an alternate outlet through their behavior.

This is very difficult for parents because their natural inclination is to quiet their teenagers, suppress their anger, and keep peace in the house. But sometimes I have to ask the parents I counsel, "Would you rather have a son yelling at you or a son overdosed on drugs? Would you rather have a sharp-tongued daughter or a pregnant one?"

Many of them quickly reply, "Neither," as if that were a realistic possibility. It's not. How many times I have observed wonderful parents in agony when they have discovered that their well-behaved and polite teenager is pregnant, on drugs, or having some other devastating problem! Please remember that unpleasant verbalization of anger is only temporary if we do our jobs in training our children to manage their anger. And you can hold on to those wonderful moments when you see your children making progress in handling their anger verbally and pleasantly. I treasure those moments in my family memories.

I also tell parents to remove the pressure from their younger teens by allowing them to verbalize their anger, then responding to them patiently and maturely. This is not being overly permissive, as long as we are handling our children's anger appropriately and leading them up the Anger Ladder. Suppressing anger is something like depressing an inflated balloon with a bulge in it. If you push the bulge in, it is going to come out somewhere else. If you try to keep your children from expressing anger, you can be sure the anger will escape at another place and another time—often with a great deal of noise.

As you keep an eye out for passive-aggressive behavior, think about your family's pressure points where it is likely to be expressed. What upsets you the most? Look for the expression right there. If you have a devoutly Christian home, look for some rebellion aimed at church and family devotional time. If you make a great fuss over yard work, look for problems in that area. If it's personal appearance, clean rooms, or loud music, those will be the targeted areas. You'll probably have to handle passive-aggressive behavior in at least two of your top three pressure points. Just remember why it's happening and how you should handle it.

Denise and Bill

Many families are likely to have both a 25-percenter and a 75-percenter, which complicates the issue even further. The siblings may experience real tension in getting along with each other; the parents may tend to favor one over the other. This comes from a lack of understanding of their children's motivation.

Tall and slender, Denise, a nursing student, came to see me one day. She sat fidgeting and looking downcast, trying to find the right words. I knew she was depressed. She finally blurted out, "I'm anorexic, Dr. Campbell. I attended a lecture on anorexia and it made me realize that I am anorexic and bulimic."

Denise began to cry. "I don't want to tell my parents because they don't think I've done much of anything right in my life as it is. Now they'll be sure to hate me."

I looked into her tear-filled brown eyes. "What are you doing that makes you think you are anorexic, Denise?"

"Well, I starve myself for as long as I can stand it. Then I eat everything in sight, take a laxative, and purge."

"How long have you been doing this?"

"About four months."

I was glad Denise had recognized her problem before coming to the point of physical damage. I felt there was a good chance of helping her through this. What we needed to discover was why she felt so negative about herself.

As I began to counsel Denise, her problem unfolded. Her older brother, Bill, was outgoing and aggressive compared to her quiet ways—75-percenter and 25-percenter.

"Ever since I can remember," Denise told me, "Bill had Mom and Dad's attention. When he was seven, he developed a life-threatening illness. I stayed with my grandparents while he was in the hospital. As lonesome as I was, I just couldn't bring myself to bother Mom and Dad at a time like that.

"When Bill came home from the hospital, he had to stay in bed for a month. I did everything I could to make him happy. I was glad we were all home together, but I felt invisible all of a sudden. Mom hardly noticed me. It wasn't that I walked around wishing I would be noticed—I just realized much later how much I craved my mother's attention.

"When Bill and I were ten and eight, Mom and Dad built a new house. There were some very hectic months for our family. I remember Bill and I were often quarreling and being punished by our father. On one of these occasions, Bill took off—just walked out the door. But I went back into the house to finish a job Mom had asked me to do."

Denise told me that she almost always gave in—not just to her brother and parents, but to anyone who crossed her—until the time when she entered high school.

"I started to change as a teenager. I still tried to keep peace at home, but I was a real character at school. In my junior year, I dated a boy who didn't amount to anything. He was just plain trouble. When my folks found out I was seeing him, they lectured me for two weeks. I never went out with him again.

"I always felt guilty if I did something that displeased my parents, and thought I was probably the worst person in the world."

In her second year of college, Denise's grades went from respectable to failing; she had developed the habit of skipping classes. She managed to keep her grades from her parents until her mother made a surprise visit to campus one day. Denise had to tell her the truth. Her angry parents moved her home and informed her that she would have to get a job and repay them the expenses for her failed attempt at a college education.

"I held two or three different jobs, finally succeeding in paying back the money, but feeling worse and worse about myself. I had no particular direction and never completed anything I started.

"All this time, Mom was directing my life. Actually, I didn't think she had done such a great job with her own life, so I resented her interference in mine. But I had no options; I couldn't afford to get a place of my own. So I had to quietly endure her interference. When I told her that I had decided to finish my education, she seemed pleased and offered to loan me the money. I refused. I knew it was now or never in my life. I had to take some kind of action soon or I would be stuck in that rut forever. So I borrowed the money, moved out of my parents' home, and started back to school.

"As soon as I made some new friends in college, I fell into the same trap of trying to settle everyone's arguments. It seemed to me that I was always there for other people, but they never seemed to be there for me. As time for graduation drew near, I panicked. I had never completed anything of importance. What if I messed up again?

"I had always been slightly overweight—or so I thought—and I started on a diet about the same time I panicked about graduation. To my surprise, I discovered I could lose weight easily. I told myself I was finally doing something successfully. That felt good—but the weight loss became an obsession."

After several weeks of intensive counseling, Denise began to understand that she was a 25-percenter. She also came to realize that her parents had not interacted with her in ways that would meet her needs. They had always loved her and didn't know that her quiet ways were deceiving. Because she didn't demand extra attention, she didn't get any. Her parents just assumed that her emotional tank was full, and they tended instead to the obvious demands of Bill, a classic 75-percenter.

Fortunately, Denise's story has a happy ending. She graduated third in her class and now works in a large hospital. She and her parents have a real relationship at last, based on love and understanding. Her parents now realize that she needs attention from them, even if she is quiet.

Do you see how easy it was for Denise's parents to control her? She wanted approval and praise, so she put all her effort into being the perfect little girl. But this finally became more than she could handle. Her lack of emotional fulfillment resulted in anger and frustration, which turned inward before finding its ultimate, destructive expression in anorexia and bulimia.

And what about Denise's spirituality? As an adolescent, she attended church and made a profession of faith. She became the exemplary teenager—until her junior year of high school when she rejected her spiritual training, considering it "baby stuff." However, she continued to attend church because she wanted her parents' approval.

Denise did, however, continue to feel a deep need for God. She was gradually drawn to prayer and Bible reading on her own, but she avoided church activities. Like most 25-percenters, she did not believe her thoughts and decisions were as important as those of more assertive persons. As she came to understand that her intelligence, thought processes, and decision-making were as effective and legitimate as those of other people, she gradually learned to depend on herself and her own opinions with confidence. She was then more secure in groups, including the church.

We need to be very careful to provide the nurture our 25-percenters need, in spirit and emotion, body and mind. Like Denise, they seem to be "low maintenance." Their "higher maintenance" siblings, like Bill, are the squeaky wheels who get all the grease. But all our children need the right "grease" at the right times. That's the art of good parenting.

Seventy-five-percenters differ from their more cautious siblings in another important way. They tend to be more global and general in their thinking, while the 25-percenters are more focused on specific detail. This means that the two types reach conclusions in different ways.

I am a 25-percenter, and my older son, David, is a 75-percenter. He and I perceive situations in our own ways and have had to learn to appreciate each other's perspective. Often I've smiled to find myself admitting that his way of handling problems is better than mine.

When David was 20 years old, he and I decided to go scuba diving in another country. On our arrival, we found that our baggage was missing. I didn't think too much about it until we realized that it was in plain sight in an airport official's office. When we brought this to the attention of the authorities, they initially denied that it was our luggage. When we insisted that it was indeed ours, they said they had no key for that office. David and I waited several hours while they "looked for" the key. As they continued to ignore our inquiries, my anger mushroomed until I was ready to explode. Complicating the whole thing for me was that their attitudes were all too reminiscent of some prejudicial ways I had been treated as a child.

David knows me pretty well, and he could see that I was about to verbally attack the officials and possibly get myself in trouble—or at least give them another excuse to hold our luggage. The training I had given David in handling anger came to fruition as he took over and said, "Dad, you are too upset. Sit down, and I'll handle this." I gladly sat down and kept my mouth shut while David kept his cool, handled it beautifully, and got our luggage back.

As a 25-percenter, I focused too much on one detail—the way we were being treated. I overreacted.

David, on the other hand, saw the whole picture and kept his perspective. We were in a foreign land where the customs differed from ours. He also maintained that this was simply an inconvenience and unworthy of spoiling the wonderful trip we had planned.

In this case, the basic 75-percenter tendencies prevailed. But, in other situations, 25-percenter traits work out best. How fortunate for the person who has learned how and when to use his strengths and when to let other people take over.

Seventy-five-percenters do not always feel deep respect for 25-percenters. Because the latter are more sensitive, feel deeply, and are more easily hurt, the 75-percenters usually consider them as weak, fragile, and easily intimidated. However, they tend to be less sensitive and also less prone to empathy and understanding of another's view. It is easy for a 75-percenter to become calloused, uncaring, selfish—eventually even a sociopath, someone marked by antisocial thoughts and behavior.

Remember that these are children who are less sensitive. They can't see the big picture as well, so they tend to blame other people. They may also have difficulty experiencing guilt. Is that a bad thing? To a point, yes, because a certain amount of guilt is necessary to develop a normal conscience.

Let's not wipe away every ounce of guilt, because our children need it to learn the difficult moral lessons. Punishment, however, can cancel out our children's guilt. When a child feels genuinely guilty about misbehaving, punishment—and especially corporal punishment—will wipe it away as clean as a slate. Let's say your five-year-old boy has broken another child's toy, simply from spite. You spank your son, and he feels a certain sense of "atonement." He committed the crime, and he paid for it. But this is not the same as feeling sympathy for the boy who now has a broken toy and experiencing that sense of personal wrong that helps us move forward as moral individuals. Punishment conditions children on the outside, but it doesn't guide them morally on the inside.

This is one of the reasons that parents must use punishment wisely and sparingly. On those occasions when children clearly feel badly about their misbehavior, please do not punish them. Let them have the experience of guilt without the interference of punishment. Your child needs to develop a normal conscience, something more and more rare today. A tremendous overuse of punishment, combined with a scarcity of unconditional love, has made this so. The result of this punishment trap is an increasing number of sociopaths who lack guilt, conscience, or any feeling for what it is like to be someone else.

Seventy-five-percenters are natural leaders. They tend to step out front and take charge. When they do so, we need them to care about their fellow citizens with understanding and good conscience.

We can't stress this enough: It's so important that we fill our children's emotional tanks. It's also important that we gently guide them toward mindsets of empathy and sympathy. If we do these things and help them learn to manage their anger maturely, we will be taking giant steps toward helping them be happy, successful, and well-loved adults who will pass on these same lessons to your grandchildren—and you will have left the world a better place than you found it.

ATTITUDES TOWARD AUTHORITY

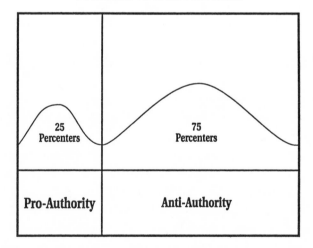

25 Percenters	**75** Percenters
Pro-Authority	**Anti-Authority**

11

Special Children, Special Problems

James was a normal, happy boy. The first seven years of his life were marked by no extraordinary circumstances or problems. When the time came for him to walk, he walked. When the time came for him to talk, he talked. Potty training was actually an easier experience than his parents expected it would be. Every milestone medical checkup was marked by smiles on the faces of doctors and parents alike. From the outside, James was coming right along.

Still, something was bothering Emily, James's mother. She couldn't quite put her finger on it, but her intuitive senses told her everything wasn't quite right. And she sensed that it had something to do with the newest setting in James's life: the classroom. There was some new kind of tension there. Others told her to relax. "He's just a growing boy," they said. "It's just normal adjustment."

Emily couldn't have realized that her son was struggling to memorize everything—every day of school. It wasn't coming as easily as it seemed to come for his first grade classmates.

James muddled along and did the best he could. But toward the end of second grade, his behavior began to decline. He often accused his mother of not really loving him, and he began to argue when asked to do simple tasks. Emily knew that some unidentified problem had manifested itself between them.

The academic problems began in third grade, when James's schoolwork grew more abstract and demanding. He was still trying to memorize everything, but his retention levels were used up. His young mind was simply out of storage space, and his grades began their downhill slide. James wanted to be a good student, and he worked even more diligently and energetically. The results were promising—for a few short weeks, until his stamina gave out. James was exhausted. It was clear that he couldn't keep up in school. Everyone was mystified because he was a bright, clever child.

James couldn't concentrate, and he struggled to remember simple tasks. And his behavior spiraled downward with his school performance—at school and at home. He showed signs of depression and, a bit more subtly, the physical symptoms of occasional twitching. James told his mother he wanted longer hair. He had figured out that by flipping his hair away from his eyes, he could hide his quirky involuntary movements. But he was also shuffling his feet and clicking the heels of his shoes together. As you might guess, James barely made it through the third grade.

As fourth grade began, the work was harder and his frustration was deeper. James was showing a defiant side now. The temper tantrums began, and at that point James's parents decided to seek counseling for him. That's how I came to meet the family.

Two things immediately were clear to me: James was a depressed child with low self-esteem. Deep down, he believed that no one cared about him. Also, he was filled with pent-up anger, especially toward authority figures. The anger was expressing itself through passive-aggressive channels as he struck out at the two controlling authorities of his young life: his parents and his teachers.

We discovered three "layered" events that were bringing about his problems. The first layer was made up of the perceptual problems that hampered his learning. For James, incoming information took a more scrambled route than for other children, and he was left confused and anxious. Thus, the second layer was one of depression, which can only worsen a learning disability as it undermines the power to concentrate. And the third layer, arising from these first two, was passive-aggressive anger. James felt powerless against his teachers and parents and was now purposely making poor grades. This was an unconscious purpose; even James didn't realize he was doing it.

By the time I saw him, James was doing poorly in every part of his life. His learning difficulties had developed into a total life problem. Also, his antiauthority attitude was out of hand. Even at his young age, he was against everything his parents stood for, including spirituality. He hated church and Sunday school and had become a constant disruption in his classes.

We began treating James for depression. We also worked with his parents' strategy in dealing with his anger. They would encourage him not to hold his anger inside where it was doing so much terrible damage to his life, but to talk it out with them so they could help him find solutions. Finally, we sought effective academic help for James.

After several months of therapy, there was no doubt that our treatment was beginning to pay off. James was more affectionate with his parents. He responded to the love that they had wanted so much to give him. He felt loved, and his self-image was clearly improving. An educational therapist was working with the passive-aggressive, anti-learning attitude that had taken firm root within James. Her process was to build a strong and positive friendship with James, then begin helping him see his schoolwork more positively. She enrolled him in the special education programs he needed, and she helped his teachers understand how to make James feel good about himself and about learning.

As the anger within James drained away and the antiauthority attitudes began to evaporate, James became more open to spiritual teaching. He was willing to go to church and enjoy his class. Physically, mentally, emotionally, and spiritually, James's life was really coming together in a gratifying way.

Friends had told Emily that "boys will be boys," and that she should simply ride out the storm. James is very fortunate that she didn't do that; some storms only become worse. Instead, his parents spent a great deal of time and therapy helping James build a better, more well-adjusted life. I see a bright future for him. I see a future adult who will honor his mother and father in life and in faith and who will show no signs of the confused, frustrated third-grade boy.

Had those problems developed because there was something wrong with the parenting? By no means. James had special problems, and they require special attention. This is a chapter about that kind of child.

Perceptual Disabilities

We know that childhood is challenging enough under the best of circumstances. There are so many adjustments to be made, so many stages to move through. What happens when a child must cope with all of those things plus a perceptual disability?

We find that these children run a strong risk of becoming rebellious against authority in their lives. Nothing seems to work, everything is a struggle, and after a while the easiest person to blame is the parent or teacher. Studies have shown that such children are prone to become juvenile delinquents, even criminals. Most distressingly, the odds of being judged delinquent are 220 percent greater for these children than for their peers without disabilities.

Children with perceptual problems are usually depressed, and depression is the one thing we desperately want to avoid in all children and teenagers. The more depressed a child is, the more angry the child becomes. Depression produces anger, and angry children are much more likely to be passive-aggressive.

When we take an already depressed, passive-aggressive child with a learning disability and superimpose the "normal" depression and passive-aggressive behavior of adolescence, the results can be explosive. The child is profoundly depressed and profoundly passive-aggressive.

Teaching the right values, of course, is like spitting into the wind when the problems are this threatening. Other foundations must first be laid. We have to help these children through the anger and depression before those reactions take root. We need to let them know that we love them unconditionally, that we're on their side as we try to help with the problem. Only then are we on the road to involving such children in genuine relationships, including the ultimate relationship, with Jesus Christ.

ADD and ADHD

We've seen a great deal of progress lately in identifying perceptual problems. The terms Attention Deficit Disorder (ADD) and Attention Deficit Hyperactive Disorder (ADHD) have entered the public vocabulary. These conditions are highly complex, but many lay people have gained significant understanding about helping such children. As you read, you may wish to refer to the graph at the end of this chapter.

I want to consider ADD and ADHD together, since they have so many similarities. Children in both categories employ inappropriate and destructive ways of handling their anger. They both involve two neurological problems—perceptual difficulties and short attention span. ADHD adds the element of hyperactivity, but hyperactivity and short attention span are so closely related that we can discuss them together.

A child with a short attention span cannot focus or concentrate long enough to learn well. His attention shifts from one distraction to another and he appears to be restless, careless, and clumsy— hyperactive.

A child with ADHD has real problems focusing on the parent. This makes it difficult for the parent to maintain the child's attention long enough to transmit positive feelings of love. Also, the parent is forced to focus primarily on the child's problems, being repeatedly drawn into the trap of expressing negative feelings to the child.

The vicious cycle continues. The angry child feels unloved and unaccepted; the parent feels frustrated for dumping anger on the child. These negative situations intensify each other. The child is angry not only at his parents but at himself. He is getting the message that he is "failing," that there's something wrong with him, that he should feel guilty. Depression deepens, and frustration ignites into rage.

I dislike giving medications to children, but sometimes they are the wise and humane way to go. The medication Ritalin (Methylphenidate) is the most well-known medication that is often appropriate for children with ADHD. It helps normalize the child's attention span so the child can focus on the parents' love. In recent years, a number of other effective medications have come into use that help children with ADD or other difficulties affecting attention span. I have seen countless children who responded to their parents' affection for the first time after taking medication. Of course, the most important factor in keeping the child's emotional tank full is the parents' unconditional love, shown with eye contact, physical contact, and focused attention. But if the child has problems receiving that love because of a short attention span, medications may help.

The other neurological factor in ADHD is perceptual. In one or more of the five senses—especially in sight and hearing—the child misperceives and misunderstands what she hears or sees. A common perceptual problem is reversal or seeing the mirror image of a letter or word. The child may see "was" instead of "saw," or a "b" instead of a "d." This condition can cause a reading difficulty called dyslexia. A child with perceptual problems also will have a hard time in accurate reception of feelings from others and will tend to receive feelings in a negative way. For this reason a child with a perceptual disability will feel that parents and other authority figures don't care. Of course, in most cases, they truly do, but the child doesn't feel it; he or she is angry and depressed.

These children are prone to depression, which is more difficult to identify in children and teens than it is in adults. It usually begins when the child is seven or eight years old and deepens to the point that it presents significant problems in the fourth grade.

Childhood depression causes decreased attention span, which, of course, worsens the already short attention span. Therefore, childhood depression decreases the child's ability to concentrate, to remember, and to think or reason clearly. It also causes great amounts of anger that can lead to passive-aggressive attitudes and behavior.

Adolescent depression is usually severe and is revealed in a variety of difficulties. Fortunately, medical people have made good progress in identifying and treating depression in both children and teenagers. Like many other doctors, I will prescribe two types of medication for such children—one to lengthen the attention span, as I mentioned earlier, and the other to control depression. I appreciate antidepressants because they are safe, non-addictive, and work in a "natural" way. By natural, I mean that they not only make the child feel good, but also correct the biochemical imbalance caused by the depression—the concentration of three hormones, norepinephrine, dopamine, and serotonin. I have seen antidepressants bring children and teenagers out of depression when nothing else could help.

Unfortunately, many people think that a child with a perceptual disability is lazy or stubborn or just plain "dumb." They fail to understand that the child does not perceive or take information from the environment as the average child does. The child's understanding of the world is distorted.

Try to imagine what life is like for such a child. She spends her day sitting in a classroom puzzling over assignments that her friends easily grasp. She is stigmatized by the teasing some of them give her, so it's a socially lonely life. Then when she comes home, her parents seem disappointed in her. They nag her about improvement, as if it were so easy. She feels that her parents don't understand her; they must not love her. And her anger builds, slowly but surely, until she emerges into adolescence with severe behavioral and emotional disorders.

Let's consider another case history.

Matt

On a nice spring day, I was enjoying my son Dale's baseball game. Across the field, I recognized a player on the opposing team as one of my patients. I had counseled with Matt and his parents several months earlier. He was 13 and I knew him as a young man with a perceptual disability; but locally, he was known as the neighborhood nuisance. I spotted one of those neighbors, Larry, in the stands, and found a seat beside him.

Matt looked our way. "Hey, Larry," he called, "which side of the base is the right side? I think I bat right-handed. The kid before me was left-handed. Should I stand where he did?"

Larry sounded irritated and impatient as he replied. "No, Matt," he said. "You should stand on the other side of the plate."

Larry turned to me. "Isn't that the dumbest thing?" he said. "Thirteen years old, and Matt doesn't know right from left!"

"Maybe he has some learning problems," I suggested.

"You're telling me! If he wasn't such a bad apple, maybe he'd learn a little better."

I didn't want to be too hard on Larry, who clearly didn't understand. I said, "There are people who don't know left from right."

"That's impossible. There's nothing wrong with him that a little willow switch wouldn't cure."

I certainly didn't see it that way. Here was a 13-year-old boy, with all the trials of adolescence, all the challenges of athletic competition—and all the problems of dealing with unsympathetic neighbors. If those stormy waters weren't tough enough to navigate, he also had to cope with an inability to comprehend basic directions. His parents and school leaders, happily enough, are helping him make satisfactory progress.

If a child like Matt has so much to overcome, the very least we can do as parents is fill his emotional tank daily. Children with perceptual disabilities have great difficulty understanding the love expressed toward them. They need extra helpings of love, physical contact, and focused attention from the important people in their lives.

Let's think about our three strategies for love and how they are affected among these children. We use eye contact, and that involves visual perception. We use physical touch, which is an overwhelmingly complex sense. And we offer focused attention as we make use of seeing, hearing, and a certain degree of logic. Perception is heavily involved in any form of love, or any medium of communication between human beings. If perceptual problems come into play, the child will not receive the messages that parents or others have sent. Understanding is distorted, and parents and children alike are frustrated.

The hardest period for parents is that time before they come to grips with the fact that their child is suffering from perceptual problems. Mom and Dad move through many stages of emotion, all of them difficult. They may begin by denying that the problem exists. They take the child for second and third opinions. They also isolate themselves, thinking that no one understands them. Next, they begin a guilt trip, agonizing over the possibility that they themselves caused the problem. They question their childrearing: "Were we too strict? Were we too easygoing?"

Then comes the anger: "We're surely not the guilty persons in this situation. We've done everything we can. It must be the doctor who doesn't know what he is talking about. And the school—they don't know how to educate properly!"

Finally, the parents start blaming each other. Meanwhile, the child sits quietly to the side and listens. Her world is already a confusing and painful one, as she is all too aware that things are not right. She watches this ever-changing emotional roller coaster and becomes afraid and depressed. At this point, parents who really want to help their child will commit themselves to counseling. There they will find hope and guidance—and their hope alone can be enough to relieve some of their child's depression and anger.

Rick

Rick, a 10-year-old, galloped into my office, an appealing child if you ever met one. Joyce, his mother, trailed behind. Rick had the first word: "I sure hope you can find out what's wrong, Dr. Campbell," he said, "because my mother worries a lot about me. Sometimes she even cries. I hate to see her do that. Maybe you can tell her something today that will make her feel better."

I thought, "What a lucky mother Joyce is."

Joyce was a single parent. Her husband had left a year ago, just about the time Rick's problem began to surface at school. She was a sincere mother who tried to do everything she could for Rick. The school teacher's words had astounded her. "There's nothing wrong with Rick other than an excess of maternal attention," she said. "You're trying too hard to compensate for the absence of his father, and you're spoiling him. He can read. All he's doing is holding out for all the attention he can get."

Imagine that—too much attention! Joyce took that advice and doled out a bit less of it, though she tutored him every evening after school. Still, nothing worked. Rick's behavior problems increased, and his grades dropped another notch—to failing. Now Joyce was serious. She sought counseling, and the two of them walked into my office.

After we evaluated Rick, I called mother and son into my office. I said, "Well, Rick, we'll just see what we can do to make you and your mom feel better."

I went over the tests with them and showed them that Rick had a visual-perceptual problem and a slight attention deficit. "But don't worry," I said, looking at Rick. "You're a bright boy, and I doubt you're too stubborn to work at reading. I think you're fine, and I'm going to work with you myself."

Rick's eyes lit up. "Listen to that, Mom. I'm not dumb after all! Now maybe you won't have to worry so much about me." It was clear that one of Rick's problems was carrying the burden of his mother's unhappiness. After beginning treatment, Rick was able to unload some of the guilt that had fed his depression.

Good News for ADHD People

• Many successful, famous people have had perceptual disabilities. When working with ADHD children, I love to tell them and their parents about well-known persons who had the problem. I emphasize my belief that ADHD and ADD are misnamed, that these children do not have a "disorder." They are normal children who happened to have been born about 150 years too late, meaning our schools offer a kind of learning that's difficult for people with perceptual difficulties.

When school attendance was not universally mandated, people with perceptual problems could learn in their own ways. I am something of a history buff, and several years ago I noticed that many of our outstanding forebears had perceptual problems. My favorite is Kit Carson. Being raised in New Mexico, I was fascinated with the way he excelled in almost every aspect of frontier life in the 1800s. Not only was he involved in most of the significant happenings in the Southwest, but he had a good heart and truly cared for Native Americans. He was well-loved by the Spanish Americans and respected by the political leaders of his day.

Several people wrote biographies of Kit Carson, and finally he wrote his autobiography. I had trouble finding this last work because it was not highly regarded. When I finally did secure a copy, I began to realize that Carson had ADHD. When I visited the Kit Carson Museum in Taos, I was spellbound as I read his notes and letters and came to understand why his autobiography was one of his few failures. His penmanship and writing style were typical of many ADHD persons I have known.

One of my favorite contemporary persons is O.D. McKee, who overcame great odds and founded McKee Bakeries of Collegedale, Tennessee, the producer of Little Debbie Snack Cakes.[1] What an inspiring story!

• Nearly every person with ADHD has some special gift or talent. Sadly, these talents are not always allowed to blossom because of the problems we have already discussed. These families need to know that there is a special strength in these children, a very positive side of that same coin. Their unique gifts will be discovered and allowed to grow only if the parents understand how to train the children to manage their anger appropriately. Only then can the defiant, antiauthority resistance of passive-aggressive behavior be prevented. It's almost always this type of anger that keeps the children from discovering and using their gifts, which are usually mechanical in nature but can bloom in every area.

• Nearly everyone has perceptual problems anyway. No one is perceptually perfect. You know the result if 10 people each tell you their version of an accident. Or you may remember that simple childhood whispering game, where one person tells the next one a message that is then passed along the line until the last person reveals what he or she heard.

The problems of most children with perceptual disabilities can be minimized if they are caught early enough. James and Rick are fortunate because their parents discovered their problems in time. Catching the problem "in time" means before the child reaches adolescence. When the condition remains untreated into adolescence, the child usually experiences much more than academic difficulty. He often has experimented with drugs, sex, stealing, running away, and may even have attempted suicide.

James, Matt, and Rick are good examples of the lives and challenges of perceptually disabled children. We can get them on the road to successful lives, but it will require our time, our patience, and a limitless love. The results, I can assure you, are well worth it all.

Linda: A Chronically Ill Child

Other problems affect children's behavior. Chronic physical ailments, for example, can create emotional and behavioral disruption. Imagine your child has a severe breathing problem. You might focus so much of your efforts on caring for the physical challenges that you unknowingly neglect the emotional ones. No matter how difficult our children's physical health challenges may be, the need for love remains the same.

You may have observed the sad pattern that takes place so frequently. A physically-impaired child grows older and becomes increasingly bitter about his problem. He feels, perhaps unconsciously, that his parents have given him medicine and health care but no loving care. He grows defiant not only toward his parents but toward all authority, and the parents, who worked so hard anyway, are broken-hearted. They wonder where they've gone wrong.

Linda's mother described her child as "a fussy baby from the very beginning." She added, "We tried everything we could think of, but we couldn't seem to make her happy. When she was three, the pediatrician discovered a chronic heart defect. Since then, our life with her has been one medical appointment after another."

"How is her physical health now?" I asked.

"It is stabilized," her father answered, "but her pregnancy certainly won't help her any."

"I see you have another child, a son," I noted, as I scanned their file. "How is his health?"

"Oh, it's perfect," Linda's mother answered. "We're so proud of Jeff. He's a fine athlete and an accomplished pianist."

"Has Linda ever developed any hobbies?" I asked.

"No," her father answered. "We've been so busy attending to her health problems that we never had the time to do much else with her. Don't get me wrong—it's not that we didn't want to. Linda has always been such a cranky kid that we could never talk her into doing anything other than going to school. And now, all of a sudden, she turns out to be pregnant! I guess it's too late."

"At least she plans to marry her baby's father next week," his wife added. "Maybe that will make her happy. We've done all we could, Dr. Campbell, but we surely went wrong somewhere." She paused before adding, "Linda's been very depressed lately. I'm relieved that we talked her into coming to see you. I sure hope you can get through to her. I can't imagine beginning a new married life with such a frame of mind."

"Why don't both of you wait outside, and let me talk with Linda," I suggested.

Curled up in a chair in the corner of the waiting room was Linda—17 years old and pregnant.

"Would you like to come in, Linda?" I asked, as I walked over to her.

"Why not? That's what they brought me here for." As she sat down in a chair in my office, she said with a frown, "I don't know what good my being here is going to do. You can't change things."

"You're right, Linda. I can't change things, but maybe in time I can help you to change the way you feel about things."

When Linda began to open up, my suspicions were confirmed. She was a classic example of the chronically ill child whose parents spent so much time caring for her physical needs that they forgot about her emotional needs.

"'Jeff can do this; Jeff can do that!' That's all I ever heard," she told me. "'Let's go to Jeff's game, Linda. It'll do you good to get out of the house. Let's go to Jeff's piano recital, Linda. Maybe you'll decide to start taking piano lessons.' And you should see the grades

Jeff makes—straight As. I made Cs and it's plenty good enough, as far as I'm concerned."

I've just begun counseling with Linda, but I feel there's hope for that troubled young lady, even with the tremendous challenges of starting a family. Her parents have always loved her deeply. They simply didn't realize they were substituting medical attention for emotional attention. Linda was angry deep inside about what seemed to her a lack of love. She struck out through rebellious attitude, then grades, then pregnancy.

We hope and pray the cycle ends here, and we work in therapy to create a fresh new start.

Three Pitfalls

In my years of treating chronically ill children and children with perceptual disabilities, I've discovered three principal pitfalls for parents. The first is the one illustrated by Linda's case: substituting medical attention for emotional fulfillment.

The second pitfall is a lack of behavioral control and firmness. These parents often feel such pity, and sometimes even blame and guilt, that they do not try to provide normal control for the child's behavior. This results in a manipulative child who uses illness to control the parents.

The third pitfall is failure to train these children to manage anger. Children with disabilities are generally more difficult to teach because they tend toward antiauthority attitudes. Their parents are then caught between pity and guilt on the one hand and their own anger on the other.

Everything we have discussed in this book certainly applies to these precious children. But their parents have little room for error. It is so easy for them to fall into the vicious cycle of rage and guilt. It is critical for these parents to understand the possible pitfalls as early as possible. The longer a difficult situation continues, the more difficult it will be to correct, especially when it involves anti-authority attitudes.

Yet, as we have seen, success can come to the child with a disability if the problem is detected and help is obtained in time. If you have a special problem child in your family, I hope that you are finding appropriate professional help and also that you are providing the unconditional love that will keep your child's emotional tank full.

I have seen innumerable children with special problems who have done beautifully. For most of these, their disabilities have become challenges that have helped to mold their character in wonderful ways.

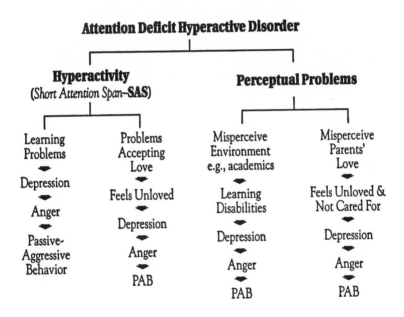

A Final Word to Parents

You and your child stand together at the threshold, looking out into a new and bewildering world. We all know the many new problems, crises, and fears that wait on the horizon.

On the other hand, it feels good to be prepared. If you've read this book carefully, you have a few tools at hand for the work that lies ahead. I would hope and pray that you'll never again think of a child's anger in the same way. I would hope and pray that you'll revisit that "Anger Ladder" and reflect upon how to help your child make the next encouraging step. I would also hope and pray that your children will see the difference in you, as you confidently and patiently work with them to help them become better, more mature creatures of God.

In time, I believe, they'll mature and return to your doorstep. They'll say, "Thanks, Mom. Thanks, Dad." They'll explain, "I can remember the anger that was inside me once, and I can remember how much we both struggled to come to grips with it. But you taught me how to handle the deep emotions that had a hold of me. You helped me work it all out verbally and pleasantly.

"You listened. You guided me. And in the end, when it came time for me to set out on my own journey, you placed in my hand a compass so that I wouldn't wander too far from the path. That compass is the example you set and the teaching you gave me. I still keep it before me. Thanks, Mom. Thanks, Dad."

My fellow parent, let me put one other word in your ear as we finish this journey of exploration together. That word is: relax! I know so many parents who are so overly conscientious that they worry themselves nearly to death. They strive with every day and every new issue to be the perfect parent—as if there were such a thing! You, my friend, will never be perfect. Neither will I, and neither will any parent you know, including your children.

Give yourself a bit of grace and mercy. Know that should you make a mistake today, should you say the wrong words tomorrow, it won't be nearly enough to ruin your children's lives. This is a marathon, not a sprint, and you have plenty of time to show your love and continue growing as a parent, even as your children continue their own growth. Don't be afraid to make mistakes because you're sure to make them—and equally sure to survive them.

You may err on the side of permissiveness, always afraid of coming down too hard; or you may err on the side of authoritarianism, straining to control every event. Wherever you fall in that vast spectrum, regardless of the precise style of parenting you choose, the main thing is to relax and enjoy your children. This stage won't last forever, and in a future day their time will be consumed with their own children. You'll look back fondly and a bit wistfully at these frantic days, so make sure you enjoy them fully—struggles and all. I can remember the day when I realized it was possible to enjoy the work of raising my children, and it was a wonderful moment for me.

In that regard, I'd like to leave you with the story of June, a 45-year-old mother of three. She came to me one day to talk about her elderly mother. June is conscientious and warm-hearted. She'd had a close relationship with her mother until the last two years, when the relationship became increasingly difficult. It seemed as if June's mother criticized her for everything. She became more and more demanding, complaining that June did not visit or call often enough. Eventually, June was spending so much time trying to care for her mother's needs that she was neglecting her own family. She had tried every tactic she could think of, including a frank discussion with her mother, but nothing had any effect on her mother's unreasonable demands.

I told June, "You're being a good daughter."

She replied, "How could I be when my mother is so disappointed in me all the time?"

I then asked her, "Have you considered what the requirements are for being a good daughter in your situation?"

June answered, "No, I've never thought about that."

I asked her to go home and make a list of what she thought was required. The next time we were scheduled to meet, we could go over that list. June told me it would be a long one.

At our next appointment, she brought me a total of six items— far fewer than she had anticipated. Visiting her mother once a week was on the list, as well as calling twice a week, sending gifts and cards for birthday and Christmas, and one or two other items. June realized she met every requirement and even exceeded them. She felt surprisingly better about herself. Why, she wasn't a bad daughter at all, but one who offered plenty of love and gave more than was required.

What remained for June? She simply needed to relax, smile and be pleasant, and also be firm, regardless of her mother's mood or attitude. This was possible in the new light of realizing that she was not in her mother's debt as a daughter. She was doing all that was required and more. It was as if a tremendous weight had been lifted from her spirit.

I asked June to make one more list. This time, I wanted her to list the things that were necessary for her to be a good parent. There's more to being a parent than an adult child, of course; the role is much more complex. Yet the same rules apply. The first list had constituted a liberating moment for June, so she took my advice seriously. She thought hard on what it took to be a good parent, and she made her list. Then she reviewed the list weekly to keep it up to date for each child.

In short, the magic worked again. June saw herself in a new and much more forgiving light. She was a good mother, and she could feel good about that fact. She could relax, smile, and be lighter in spirit without the anxiety of trying to live up to some undefined and unreachable standard. Best of all, June found herself enjoying each of her children more than ever before. She could appreciate what was unique and special about each of them.

As you close this book, why not open a notebook? Make your own list and follow your heart in what parenting means to you. What is required of you? What isn't required? Make your list and check it more than twice. Reread this book regularly, reviewing the sections that are most helpful to you. Keep a close account of your parenting that will tell you that you're doing all you can, and it's OK to relax and enjoy the life of a parent.

By coming this far with me, even to the last page, you've made a remarkable statement about yourself. You want to be the best parent you can be, and I have no doubt you're much closer to that goal than you suspect. Simply remember to love your children, let them know you love them, and be sure you know you're loved by God. Between the love of that eternal Parent and the love of the children before us, we have all that we need to make this life—and the future of our children—strong and vibrant. May God walk with you on that journey.

A Conversation with Dr. Campbell

Q: What is the worst way to handle anger?

A: Very clearly, it's the passive-aggressive way, which can add up to the self-destruction of any person's life.

The most dangerous thing about passive-aggressive behavior is that it begins subconsciously—that is, hidden from one's conscious thoughts. But if a child has no training in anger management, passive-aggressive behavior can become a conscious course. Passive-aggressive behavior, as discussed in chapter 6 of this book, is the subconscious determination to do exactly the opposite of what one should do. The issue is authority and the refusal to follow it, particularly with parents and teachers. As a matter of fact, the specific objective is to upset that authority figure.

If you consider this idea, you'll realize that passive-aggressive behavior is extremely difficult to eliminate once it has taken root. The person under its influence simply subverts every desire of the authority figure who tries to bring order. Both people end up frustrated and angry. You can imagine how disordered and chaotic such a life becomes. Yet today, we find this behavior has become so common that it's almost the social and cultural status quo—and a likely destination for those whose parents fail to train their children in anger management. That's reason enough for you to read this book carefully.

You can identify passive-aggressive behavior in three different ways, shown in the following example of Julie, a sharp teenage girl.

- It makes no rational sense. Julie, who has no learning disabilities, makes failing grades, even though she is capable of passing with ease.
- No response strategy is successful. Why? Because the purpose of the passive-aggressive behavior is to upset you, the authority figure. God help the parent and child when this happens. Julie's parents try every response—tutors, supervised study, restrictions, reasoning. Strategies are irrelevant because they are rational, and passive-aggressive behavior is not rational.
- The passive-aggressive person is the ultimate victim. Authority figures are targeted, but the one behaving this way is the one who will suffer. Julie is striking out at her parents and teachers by failing, but she harms her own future prospects by dropping out of high school—and the pain keeps coming. As a young adult, Julie will be constitutionally prone to strike out at authority figures, and she will cause more problems for herself. The pattern, unless arrested, will carry forward. Her attempts at social life, marriage, parenting, and career will be severely damaged by passive-aggressive behavior. She will keep targeting bosses, teachers, husbands, and pastors, and she will keep hurting herself much more than anyone else.

The cycle ends only when she learns to handle her anger and, perhaps in therapy, work through all its complications over the years.

Q: How does a child become passive-aggressive?

A: Any child will develop a passive-aggressive anger response if he or she isn't trained to manage anger maturely. However, the surest way to push children toward this dysfunction is to dump our own anger on them. Children have two profound fears:

- Unmet emotional needs, or, as we say in this book, an empty emotional tank;
- Parental anger.

Children have no defense against either problem. When we dump our anger on them, it penetrates deep into the soft soil of their psyches, and the seeds lie there until finally they bear bitter fruit in terms of behavior. They will take various actions without quite realizing their objective: to upset parents, teachers, employers, policemen, spouses, or anyone who has any level of control. And remember, an authority is not only someone to whom we are responsible but for whom we are responsible. That's why spouses must take note.

Q: Why are most children handling their anger so poorly today? And why is it getting worse?

A: A complex question requires a complex answer.

First of all, our culture has experienced a dramatic change in the last 30 years, especially in the last 10. We've slowly changed from pro-authority to strong antiauthority in orientation—a truly passive-aggressive society. Until the last 10 years, our culture did a good job helping parents train their children to handle anger maturely. Our television reflects what I'm talking about. We remember shows like "Leave It to Beaver" and "The Andy Griffith Show" that had moral lessons written into them. You can watch any number of those episodes and see how children are encouraged to handle anger maturely.

But look at our contemporary programs: almost every example of anger management is inappropriate and self-defeating. The wise parent realizes that her culture is no longer "watching her back"; it actually serves as a bad influence, and Mom and Dad must take the utmost care to teach all the right lessons. It can be done, but parents must learn how. That is what this book is all about.

Q: What is the best way to handle anger?
A: Three things:
• express it verbally,
• express it pleasantly,
• and resolve the anger with those to whom it was directed.

That third point has a disclaimer. In some cases, we can't resolve the anger with the person involved. Instead, we must find ways to resolve it within ourselves. If these three prongs of good anger management are new to you, you can be certain your child doesn't know about them. Please don't expect your child to handle anger in the right ways, because, to paraphrase the apostle Paul in Romans 10:14, how will they know without a teacher? We must know what to teach them, then teach it clearly.

Q: If children cannot be expected to handle their anger verbally and pleasantly and to resolve it, how should we expect them to handle anger?

A: All children start out handling their anger in the natural way—verbally and unpleasantly. That's the human starting point, and we need to expect that. If we train children correctly, they will gradually learn to manage anger maturely: verbally and pleasantly. They will acquire the ability to actually resolve the anger so that it doesn't fester within them. Our goal is to train them to go from handling anger verbally and unpleasantly to verbally and pleasantly. Without training, they will eventually be oversuppressed and they will begin expressing it in behavior. Nor will they learn to resolve their anger, which is one of the most important goals of good mental health. The "finish line" for learning to handle anger maturely, in my observation, should be around the age of 17. As you can see, this is no simple two-week course.

Q: I have an adult child. I failed in my training, and now he's passive-aggressive. My son never follows through with anything, always blames others for anything wrong, and refuses to take responsibility for his own behavior. He constantly lies and breaks promises. Is there anything I can do at this late date?

A: This is a very common question, and I applaud the honesty of all who ask it. It's heartbreaking to live with a troubled adult child—and it happens so frequently. You might succeed in every area of training except the one. If you fail to teach your child to handle hanger, you will see the sad developments as life progresses. Worst of all, there will be little you can do at that point.

Remember that the purpose of passive-aggressive behavior is to upset the authority figure. No matter what you do to correct the behavior, nothing will work. Even a professional counselor will struggle to deal with this problem in adults because the counselor is only one more authority figure.

What can you do? Go to an experienced counselor who understands this type of behavioral problem. Seek advice on how you should respond in your specific circumstances.

What should you not do? The worst approach is direct confrontation. Never approach your son or daughter and challenge your adult child to change.

Q: I'm still confused about what you mean by "ventilation."

A: Again, thank you for asking that question. Ventilation is one of the most difficult concepts to explain. There are appropriate and inappropriate ways for children to express anger. Ventilation is one of the inappropriate ways. To vent is to "let it all hang out." We wreak havoc around us by fully ventilating, or releasing, our angry emotions.

The child's reasons for venting are all inappropriate. For example, she vents to manipulate the parent. She will use histrionics to wear down a tired mother until Mom finally gives in and says, "Go ahead! Do what you want."

Frequently, the child is trying to use ventilation to irritate the parent to such an extent that the parent will finally say, out of pure frustration, "all right, go ahead and do it!" The child may also use ventilation to avoid taking responsibility for his own behavior and to distract the parent from enforcing legitimate behavior.

What is the parent to do when a child uses ventilation? Handle it like any other misbehavior. We should ask ourselves the appropriate question, beginning with, "What does this child need?" Then we go on from there. Please remember that we cannot train a child to handle anger maturely when the child is ventilating. We want the child to express anger verbally with a legitimate reason. That's when good training can occur.

Q: OK, let's say my child is not ventilating or being aggressive, and she has a legitimate reason for bringing her anger to me. How do I handle it then, especially if she is unpleasantly loud?

A: What you have described is exactly what we want. When the child has a real reason for expressing anger verbally, and she is not ventilating and being aggressive—she's not trying to hurt us, verbally or physically—we should rejoice. This may not be what you want to hear, but it's certainly what we need to understand. Here's why.

We have, in these conditions, a "teachable moment." First, we carefully listen to her. She shares exactly why she is angry. These things are difficult and unpleasant for you to hear, and your every instinct is to stifle your child's expression—or to be argumentative. But maturity doesn't dictate those reactions; it dictates that you remain calm and pleasant. When your child has expressed (discharged) her anger, she is calmer and more ready to be trained. Both of you are under emotional control. Then we have three objectives:

- First, we want to affirm the child. Bringing her anger to you was the right thing to do. This is especially important for the 25-percenter (see chapter 10). Many children have been taught that bringing anger to parents is misbehavior. Instead, I like to say something like this: "I'm glad you brought your anger to me, honey. When you're happy, I want to know it; when you're sad, I want to know that, too. And when you're angry, it's no different. So thank you for bringing your anger to me." If your children can't bring their anger to you, where can they take it? Nowhere, so it takes root within them.
- Second, we want to praise the child. She expressed it verbally, not behaviorally. I like to say something like: "I'm proud of the way you handled your anger, son. You didn't take it out on your little brother. You didn't take it out on the dog. You didn't slam the door. You didn't try to confuse me with a bunch of meaningless explanations. You brought your anger to me and simply told me how you felt about it. That's great."
- Third, we want to boost her to the next rung on the Anger Ladder. It's a long climb from the most immature anger responses to the best and wisest (see the illustration on page 76). And it's difficult for parents to be patient and remember

their child can only climb one rung at a time. But we have the advantage of knowing what that next step should be. For example, if your child has a tendency to call you a name when he expresses his anger verbally, this is a good place to take the next step. Simply make the request. You might say, "I appreciate your bringing your anger to me, but from now on, I'm hoping you won't call me names. OK" You might add, "You'll be showing some real maturity by avoiding that." Always point out that climbing to the next rung is mature and worthy of applause.

There's no guarantee that your child will do that. Sometimes he or she will take the step, sometimes not. It may take a day, a week, or a month. But when the child is emotionally ready and mature enough, he or she will indeed move upward. Don't be discouraged, because it may be three steps up, two steps down, then stuck for a while. But if we show patience and handle ourselves well while training them, they will enter that one normal passive-aggressive stage, then emerge to a new and adult-like maturity around the age of 17. What a blessing and a time for celebration!

Q: Isn't it disrespectful for a child to express anger verbally?
A: Your excellent question brings to light one of the most misunderstood aspects of parenting. To be unpleasant is not to be disrespectful.

There are only two ways to express anger—verbally and behaviorally. And behavioral responses are simply unacceptable (passive-aggressive being the worst). We'd love for the child to express anger verbally and pleasantly, but at a young age it's simply not part of a child's skill set. For that matter, how many adults do you see express anger verbally and pleasantly? We can't expect small children to do automatically what adults do only rarely and after a long process of maturation. Keep the visual image of the ladder in mind.

One way to help yourself deal with this problem is to ask yourself whether your child is normally respectful or disrespectful. Assuming that you're filling your child's emotional needs, I would predict that your child is respectful most of the time. Remind yourself of this when your child is expressing anger verbally. This will help you to maintain your own self-control and prevent you from dumping your anger on your child.

The choice is yours: you can consider your child's verbally unpleasant words as disrespectful, suppress it, and watch the anger re-emerge in passive-aggressive behavior; or you can be patient with an appropriate level of verbal anger, knowing that it's being discharged and settled now and forever. I'm quite serious about that choice—please don't bring in the issue of respect.

Q: I have an anger problem of my own. What can I do to improve my self-control?

A: Join the crowd, my friend; we all struggle with anger.

There are various steps we can take to manage our own anger better. My very favorite is a suggestion that has helped thousands of parents. I call it the Anger Diary. Every night, before turning in, jot down your thoughts in that journal. How have you handled your anger as a parent during the preceding day? Write it down while it's fresh in your memory.

Don't use this as a guilt party. Be fair with yourself and write down the good things you did, too—just as I've told you to thank your child for what he did right. If you didn't scream, if you didn't slam doors, and if you didn't say words you regret, those are matters for which to be thankful. But what could you have done better? Think of a plan for tomorrow. If this same issue arises, you'll be better prepared for it. You'll find much more strength and self-control in having thought things through beforehand.

Promise yourself, your child, and God that you will do a better job for the next 24 hours. In that short a period, almost anyone can keep a commitment.

Then, the next day—24 hours later—you can check the log and see how it all worked out. Again you can commend yourself for the good, encourage yourself for the better, and fortify your resolve for another 24 hours of improved parenting.

This idea can be a great help to you, but if the problems run a little deeper—if you are genuinely concerned about your temper and your lack of self-control—then you'll want to seek help from a professional counselor.

Q: Are there any other practical steps or handy tips you can suggest?

A: Yes; you may be familiar with a little device known as self-talk. Let's consider how you might use it in the case of anger.

When your child is expressing anger verbally, we're aware of our need to set a good example and not give in to our own anger. As long as your child isn't venting or using aggression, and assuming he has a real reason for anger, the fact is that he's not misbehaving. He's simply angry. Therefore, you might say to yourself (not to the child), "Attaboy, son, let it all hang out. Let the anger flow because once you let it go, I've succeeded."

And that's no exaggeration. As long as the anger is inside, especially in a teenager, the whole atmosphere of your home will be affected. But when the anger is properly and verbally expressed, the parent remains in control. So as your child expresses his anger, allow your imagination to wander down the road a bit and consider how that anger might finally emerge if left inside—in the form of drugs, rebellion, and misbehavior of all kinds. Use self-talk to keep yourself on track.

Q: Why can't a parent simply instruct a child how to handle anger and make him do it right?

A: That is exactly what most parents are naturally inclined to do. And that is exactly why very few people manage their anger maturely.

Children are immature, and they'll handle their anger accordingly until they're taught better methods. Anger management is a maturational process and cannot be rushed. If we expect children to manage their anger maturely, then punish them when they fail, we're not training them. Negative reinforcement forces suppression, and we've seen where that leads. It would be wonderfully easy to do anger training if it were only a matter of punishment and rewards.

It's not a sprint, but a marathon run; be patient. Real maturity is like a precious jewel, shining before the world, and it's well worth the wait. You can help or you can hamper—but you can't rush. I hope you'll settle in for the duration, keep a copy of this book handy, and reaffirm to yourself—and perhaps your spouse—the hard truths about anger and the hopeful strategies for managing it.

Q: You say that the primary lifetime threat to the child is his or her own anger. Why is this true?

A: People tend to think we're defined by our choices—the conscious decisions we make along the road of life.

But that's quite simply a myth. Subconscious motivations are the primary determinants in the qualities of our lives. We all have positive and negative motivations within us. We're motivated deep within our subconscious to help people and to have a positive influence on the world—to leave it a better place. We're motivated to tell the truth, to keep our promises, and to assume responsibility for our behavior.

But we're also subconsciously motivated to do precisely the opposite. There are compulsions within us to be untruthful, to break promises, and to pass off the blame. What causes the negative subconscious compulsions? The way we manage our anger. When anger, prevented from verbal and conscious resolution, has burrowed deep within you, it takes its toll on your subconscious urges. It's an irrational force, one that moves toward chaos and rebellion. Passive-aggressive people don't know why they strike out at others in the ways they do. Their anger has rewired them deep within their human circuitry.

Reflect on that insight, and I believe you'll see why I say that anger is our primary life threat. It is more pervasive than cancer or any other disease—it is a cancer of the soul. We cannot afford to let it consume the fragile psyches of our children with all their potential for wholesome goodness in this world.

We all need help in training our children in the way they should go. It's my hope that this book is helpful to you. It's my prayer that God will be your guide. But in the end, you are the parent. You are the greatest influence, the most powerful shaper and model that your child will ever have. That's an awesome responsibility—but it pays off magnificently. May your children grow wise and mature, solid in integrity and in full possession of self-control. In that way, you will have impacted the world of the future in a way that will bring God to smile and say, "Well done, good and faithful servant."

Notes

Chapter 1

1. Neil Clark Warren, *Make Anger Your Ally* (Colorado Springs: Focus on the Family Publishing, 1990), 55, 77.
2. Ibid., 121.
3. Ibid., 97.

Chapter 2

1. Thomas Sowell, "Who Says It's Hopeless?" *Reader's Digest*, June 1994, 180.
2. Benjamin Spock, *A Better World for Our Children* (Bethesda: National Press Books, 1994).
3. Neil Clark Warren, *Make Anger Your Ally* (Colorado Springs: Focus on the Family Publishing, 1990), 8.

Chapter 3

1. "Burdened Teens Feel Estranged From Adults," *The Chattanooga Times*, 14 July 1994.
2. Stuart Goldman, "Murder as Therapy," *National Review* 45, 29 November 1993, 44–46.

Chapter 4

1. Adapted from *How to Really Love Your Child* (Colorado Springs: Victor, 2003), chapter 3.
2. David Seamands, *Healing for Damaged Emotions* (Colorado Springs: Victor, 2002), 61.
3. Ibid., 63–64.
4. David Seamands, *Putting Away Childish Things* (Wheaton, IL: Victor Books, 1982), 33.
5. Neil Clark Warren, *Make Anger Your Ally* (Colorado Springs: Focus on the Family Publishing, 1990), 123.
6. Ibid., 123–124.
7. Ibid., 125.

Chapter 5

1. Andrew D. Lester, *Coping with Anger: A Christian Guide* (Philadelphia: The Westminster Press, 1983), 34–35.
2. Carol Travis, *Anger: The Misunderstood Emotion* (New York: Simon and Schuster, 1989), 47.
3. "The Traits of Wrath in Men and Women," *USA Today*, 11 August 1994.
4. Meg Eastman, *Taming the Dragon in Your Child* (New York: John Wiley and Sons, 1994), 4.

Chapter 6

1. Ruth N. Koch and Kenneth C. Haugk, *Speaking the Truth in Love: How to Be an Assertive Christian* (St. Louis: Stephen Ministries, 1992), 16–17, 19.
2. Ibid., 22.

Chapter 7

1. Leonard D. Eron, *Reason to Hope: A Psychosocial Perspective on Violence and Youth*, (Washington, D.C.: American Psychological Association, 1994).
2. Meg Eastman, *Taming the Dragon in Your Child* (New York: John Wiley and Sons, 1994), 187–188.
3. Andrew D. Lester, *Coping with Your Anger* (Philadelphia: The Westminster Press, 1983), 59.

4. Howard S. Friedman and Stephany Booth-Kersley, "The Disease-Prone Personality: A Meta-Analytic View of the Construct," *American Psychologist* 42, 1987, 539–55.

5. Carol Travis, *Anger: The Misunderstood Emotion* (New York: Simon and Schuster, 1989), 129.

6. Ibid., 131–42.

7. Ibid., 137.

8. Ibid., 139–41.

9. Ibid., 146.

Chapter 9

1. Ellen Goodman, "A Mom Fights Media Madness," *Family Circle*, 14 March 1995, 135.

2. Gladys Hunt, *Honey for a Child's Heart* (Grand Rapids: Zondervan Publishing House, 1989).

3. William Kilpatrick and Gregory and Suzanne M. Wolfe, *Books That Build Character: A Guide to Teaching Your Child Moral Values through Stories* (New York: Simon and Schuster, Inc., 1994).

4. William Bennett, *The Book of Virtues: A Treasury of Great Moral Stories* (New York: Simon and Schuster, Inc., 1993).

5. Martin E. Seligman, *Learned Optimism* (New York: Simon and Schuster, Inc., 1980).

6. Thomas Gordon, *Parent Effectiveness Training* (New York: David McKay, Inc., 1970).

7. Meg Eastman, *Taming the Dragon in Your Child* (New York: John Wiley and Sons, 1994).

Chapter 11

1. C.A. Oliphant, *Sweet Success* (Cleveland, Tenn.: Sundial Press, 1994).